The Origin of the Germans

On the Method of Settlement Archaeology

by

Gustaf Kossinna

with Supplements and 9 Maps

Translated by Trevor Sutcliffe

Argent Ardor
2023

Original translation of *Die Herkunft der Germanen: Zur Methode der Siedlungsarchäologie*
Mannus-Bibliothek No. 6

Published in the United States by Argent Ardor, LLC

Copyright © 2023 Trevor J. Sutcliffe

This version translated from the 2nd edition published by Curt Kabitzsch, Leipzig, 1920
First edition published by Curt Kabitzsch, Würzburg, 1911

All rights reserved.

ISBN: 9798857566749

Gustaf Kossinna holding a ceramic vessel, circa 1925

TRANSLATOR'S PREFACE

As results from the new discipline of archaeogenetics have flown in over the past decade, a renewed spotlight has been shone upon the importance of mass migrations in shaping the ethnocultural landscape of human populations in prehistoric Europe. These findings and the resulting paradigm shift have evinced a palpable level of anxiety among many researchers of prehistory, with archaeologists often leading the pack in expressing apprehension over such results, not least due to concerns over any potential validation of the works of Gustaf Kossinna and his *siedlungsarchäologische Methode* — the method of settlement archaeology presented in this very booklet. For some curious observers, a natural response to such furor may be to seek out Kossinna's work to investigate why this German prehistorian continues to haunt the field of archaeology like a ghost, but alas, none of Kossinna's works have until now been translated to English. As such, for those in the English-speaking world who lack proficiency in the German language, insights into Kossinna's views and methods could only be gleaned from secondary sources, and often only from authors with an unfavorable view of Kossinna, largely due to the political use of his research and methods during the National Socialist period of German history, which began not long after Kossinna's death in 1931. With the aim of rectifying this unsatisfactory situation, it seemed sensible to start by providing a translation of this most seminal 1911 work, as it not only serves as a solid introduction to Kossinna's viewpoints and methods, but also provides insights into his disputes with some of his contemporaries which remain surprisingly relevant to the scientific debates of today.

As is mentioned in Kossinna's forward, this 1920 second edition was originally published as a reprint of the first edition, followed by supplemental commentary and a list of unincorporated changes. These supplements and changes were presented according to page number and, in the case of the latter, also by line number from the top or bottom of the page. Here I have incorporated all of these changes into the main body of the text for the reader's convenience. However, for those who may be interested in how Kossinna's understanding had evolved over the course of that decade, I also provide the segments of the text which have been replaced where the unincorporated changes would otherwise have been located. For the sake of completeness, I also follow that list of changes with my own brief discussion of the changes Kossinna made to the table on page

29, which is arguably the centerpiece of the work, along with some additional commentary; this section is clearly marked with the heading "Translator's Note." Kossinna's footnotes are largely provided in the format that he presented them, however in some cases I have expanded certain abbreviations or added some additional bibliographic information. I have also herein maintained Kossinna's convention of presenting surnames in all capital letters. The table and included maps have all been carefully digitally processed to ensure the highest possible quality of representation, and the English text within them was formed from the original lettering so that they are aesthetically identical to how they might have looked had the work been originally published in English.

Throughout the text, the choice was made to translate the German term *indogermanische* to "Indo-Germanic," even though Indo-European has clearly long been the overwhelmingly dominant term in the English-speaking world. This was done not only because Indo-Germanic is the literal translation of the term which remains dominant in the German-speaking world, but also because its use seems particularly apt within the context of this booklet, as well as with respect to Kossinna's views on the origin of the Proto-Indo-Europeans (or as I refer to them here, the Proto-Indo-Germanics). This booklet was of course not Kossinna's final word on either the question of the origin of the Germanics or on the Indo-European question, and we hope to bring you additional translations of Kossinna's writings on those subjects in the future, but without further ado, I proudly present you with the first English translation of this classic work from Gustaf Kossinna.

FOREWARD

This booklet was a composition for a special occasion when it was first published, intended for distribution at the third general meeting of the Society for German Prehistory in Koblenz in August 1911. The not small amount of copies then sold out surprisingly quickly. I had to keep putting off organizing a new edition, for which the publisher had been asking for many years, because ongoing work and new writings were taking up all of my time. For it was always my intention, in order to share some of that writing, to not just dedicate a small special issue of the *Mannus* library to the "Method of Settlement Archaeology," but to ultimately deal with the "Origin of the Germanics" on a larger scale. The latter seems all the more necessary to me now that a year ago I arrived at a new, more in-depth understanding of the Germanic question, which both eliminates the main objections of the latest linguistic research, and also solves some of the riddles which, on the anthropological and archaeological side, stood in the way of my earlier understanding (and even more so the understanding of other researchers). I have already communicated my new view in my winter lectures of 1919/20 on the Indo-Germanics, and it was also at least alluded to in a lecture that was printed in *Mannus* 11/12 (pp. 249 ff.). However, I do not yet see the possibility of gaining time to present this conception in book form within the near future, and so I finally gave in to the publisher's insistence that at least one reprint of the first edition be allowed, despite my great reluctance. However, I emphatically refer the reader to the completely new table (page 29), to the supplements and changes (page 32), and to the added maps, of which those on page 35 (Early Iron Age of the East Germanics), page 36 (Saale area), and page 43 (Bronze Age periods) have now been completely reworked by me.

G. K.

*There are many who see,
but few who notice.*
Machiavelli

I.

From among the circle of scholars who as devoted students were close to the renowned Germanist and archaeologist Karl MÜLLENHOFF in Berlin — a fortune which was granted to me at the end of the 1870s — hardly a one has dedicated himself to our master's most intimate field of study, the question of the origin and the earliest development of our people. Yet it was already clear to me as a student that it had to be my life's work to follow in my teacher's very personal footsteps. While compiling the prerequisite collection of historical and linguistic material for solving such a riddle, I very quickly realized that the historical-philological and linguistic realities could not by themselves lead to the goal that I had set for myself, nor could they even serve as the primary means by which to achieve it. In my younger years, in addition to geography and settlement studies, I began to draw prehistoric archaeology, and later also anthropology, into the narrow circle of my studies. And when, in the beginning of the 1880s, it became increasingly clear to all critical minds whose vision was not limited to narrow horizons that Europe was the original homeland of the Indo-Germanics, the unsolved problems of the Indo-Germanic age of the European nations gripped me with a hold that has never loosened.

For all of these questions, prehistoric archaeology became a most splendid foundation for me, indeed really the only reliable guide, because it is the only science that through its subject matter leads us right into the middle of the distant past, while from any of the other relevant sciences only unclear ideas can be gained and only uncertain conclusions can be drawn. It was only a matter of finding the right stretch of land that served as the home of a tribe, of a people, of an ethnic group — the Proto-Indo-Germanic people, for example — then its cultural history could be extracted merely from the soil of the determined area, or, if that had already happened in part, immediately inferred from the finds that were already excavated from the soil, — provided that a strict chronology of the historical periods, at first relative, then absolute, had already been established for such lands. Epoch-making for all time was the first step in this direction by Oscar MONTELIUS with his work on the determination of the chronology of the Scandinavian Bronze Age in the year 1885.

The path forward had thus been cleared for me. I then devised my current method, erected on a purely archaeological foundation, with which I intended to lead my ethnographic research to new goals. But it was not until 1895 that I made my first attempt, which was dedicated to the origin of the Germanics and their migrations within Central Europe prior to the beginning of the historical tradition[1]. In the years that followed, the problems of the Indo-Germanics, and, in connection with them, the prehistories of most of the European peoples of today, were dealt with numerous times, each time according to the same more and more refined method[2].

It has often been suggested to me from various quarters that I should present this method briefly and in context. In complying with this request, I will immediately add an individual case of its practical application to the presentation of the method, and I will choose the same topic with which I first ventured in this direction in 1895, because it is a very excellent instructional example to explain,

---

[1] *Zeitschrift des Vereins für Volkskunde* VI, pp. 1 ff.; also excerpts from the *Korrespondenzblatt der Deutschen anthropologischen Gesellschaft* 1895, pp. 109 ff.; Addendum 1896, pp. 30 ff.

[2] 1. "Die indogermanische Frage archäologisch beantwortet" (The Indo-Germanic Question Answered Archaeologically), *Zeitschrift für Ethnologie* 1902, pp. 161 ff.

2. "Der Ursprung der Urfinnen und Urindogermanen und ihre Ausbreitung nach dem Osten" (The Origin of the Proto-Finns and Proto-Indo-Germanics and their Expansion to the East), *Mannus, Zeitschrift für Vorgeschichte*. Bd. I. 1909, pp. 17 ff., pp. 225 ff.; Bd. II. 1910, pp. 59 ff.

3. "Eingeritzte Zeichnungen in Steinkistengräbern" (Carved Drawings in Stone Cist Graves), *Korrespondenzblatt des Gesamtvereins der deutschen Geschichts- und Altertumsvereine*, Bd. 56, 1908, pp. 343 ff., (about the origin of the Germanics and the Celts).

4. "Die Grenzen der Kelten und Germanen in der Latène-Zeit" (The Boundaries of the Celts and Germanics in the La Tène Period), *Korrespondenzblatt der Deutschen Gesellschaft für Anthropologie* 1907, pp. 57 ff.

5. "Verzierte Lanzenspitzen als Kennzeichen der Ostgermanen" (Decorated Lance Tips as a Hallmark of the East Germanics), *Zeitschrift für Ethnologie* 1905, pp. 371 ff.; addendum pp. 596 ff.

6. "Germanische Mäanderurnen" (Germanic Meander Urns), *Korrespondenzblatt der Deutschen Gesellschaft für Anthropologie* 1907, pp. 165 f.

through its application to this question, the method itself.

This method makes use of reasoning by analogy insofar as it casts a light upon the darkness of the primeval times through inferences drawn from the clarity of the present, or from those epochs that, while still ancient, are nevertheless distinguished by richness of lore and legend. It illuminates the prehistoric times through times which stand in the light of history; preferably starting first with the illumination of the prehistoric periods which immediately preceded the dawn of history through the adjacent period of protohistory. This thread of knowledge of prehistoric times that has been spun in this way, especially the knowledge of the way in which prehistoric facts are characteristically reflected in the archaeological finds, above all the way that ethnic tribes reveal themselves en bloc and within each of their specific confines to the studied archaeologist, let's not drop this thread again, but instead continue to weave it back further into earlier and earlier ages.

The guiding principle, the correctness of which has been demonstrated a thousand times for the early historical ages, which has always proven itself anew, and which therefore must also be equally as valid for both the closely adjacent as well as for the most distant prehistoric periods, is the following: sharply delimited archaeological cultural provinces coincide at all times with very specific ethnic groups or ethnic tribes.

Surprisingly, there are still scholars and even prehistorians who have so poorly comprehended what the archaeological material tells us that they constantly deny that the expansion and evolution of cultures can be used to draw conclusions about ethnic migrations: in contrast to such a view, the certainty of the opposite is then emphasized with absolute conviction. Any true expert can clearly discern each of the following from the archaeological record: wherever the Vikings had established settlements, be it in Normandy, in the British Isles, or in Russia; when the Norwegians settled Iceland; how far westward into central and northern Germany the Wendish populations had advanced during the Middle Ages; wherever the Germanics had invaded during the so-called Germanic *Völkerwanderung*, and even which Germanic tribes come into question in each case, for example, when it comes to Italy, whether we are dealing with the Ostrogoths or the Longobards; how the main Germanic tribes had been divided geographically in eastern Germany, and when and to what extent each of them had left their country during the Völkerwanderung; how the respective border between East Germanic and West Germanic tribes had changed in the first centuries after Christ; how in the last centuries before Christ the Celtic population of western-central Germany had receded before the advance of the Germanics; and conversely, how since the 5th century BC the stream of Gallic migration had poured out of northern France towards southern Germany and then headed further east; how far since the 8th century BC the Scythians had extended their rule over lands from southern Russia to Transylvania, Hungary, Galicia, and even sporadically to eastern Germany; where in Sicily and Italy or on the Black Sea there had been Hellenic colonies; and so on and so forth. All of that can be discerned not just roughly or spoken of in general terms, but determined with precision down to the smallest detail, far more precisely in terms of dates and locations than anything the scribes, from whichever era, have been able to tell us. Indeed, even if we didn't know the least bit about all of these ethnic migrations from documented history, these events would necessarily have to be deduced just from their artifacts alone.

So if our principle "cultural areas are ethnic areas" is unconditionally valid for the historical eras, for the early historical times, and for the times lying on the cusp of prehistory, then it is completely incomprehensible where some scholars — especially those who don't know the field of prehistory or only know it from afar — get the courage to reject applying this principle to the prehistoric periods without any valid justification, and thereby at the same time find it convenient to simply dismiss my research and my results. Nevertheless, prehistory and history can no longer be separated, even less so than Orient and Occident. On the contrary: every day prehistory teaches us more and more how little the man of prehistoric times differed from the man of early history, and even from the man of modern times. This should also be emphasized as we turn to face off against such adversaries as Eduard MEYER, Otto SCHRADER, and Moriz HÖRNES.

What Eduard MEYER brought forth in the first edition of his *Geschichte des Altertums* (The History of Antiquity) against the equation "cultural provinces are ethnic tribes" was so unsound that it was easy for me, on the occasion of my lecture in the year 1895 on the Germanic expansion[1], to demonstrate the unworthiness of his statements, for example in cases where he uses medieval architectural styles as a basis for drawing parallels. Nevertheless, in the second edition of the work, the author returned to this subject without removing any of

---

[1] *Zeitschrift des Vereins für Volkskunde* 1896, p. 3.

the superficiality of consideration of the kind I had characterized in order to make his propositions more plausible[1]. MEYER also takes advantage of every opportunity to emphasize again and again that the cultures that are established through archaeological finds do not represent individual ethnic groups. So he says in his treatment of Egypt (p. 55): "Written testimony almost never gives us a reliable answer to ethnographic questions." Indeed, I would like to know exactly who and what he had in mind when he declared in his introductory volume on archaeology (p. 164): the main value of the "prehistoric" finds lies in the fact "that through the energetic and constantly advancing work of important researchers, it has become possible to connect the individual groups of artifacts with historically known cultures, and even in some cases with singular, tangibly distinct ethnic groups, and to thereby gain new insights into their development." Yet wheresoever he deals with these questions in specific cases, be it in Egypt, in Asia Minor, in Southeastern Europe, in Northern Europe, on the Indo-Germanic question, and so on[2], he behaves dismissively, but without ever providing counter-evidence; on the contrary, like all opponents of my method, he has contented himself with generalized, albeit long-winded trains of thought which, as we have just seen, often enough lead to complete platitudes. It is really nothing new, especially not for the prehistorian, that a large ethnic group, or even a smaller ethnic group never has a completely uniform culture within all of its constituent divisions, but that the tribes and even the "*gaue*," to repeat MEYER's expression, display their own shades of the broader culture. However, never has a tribe within an ethnic group comprehensively adopted the entire culture of a foreign people which is completely absent in any of the other tribes of that first ethnic group. It would then cease to be a member of that ethnic group. The fact of the distinct shades of culture of the separate tribes within ethnic groups speaks not in favor of MEYER, but only in favor of me, and completely against MEYER.

I am certainly happy to bow before the outstanding achievement that MEYER's *Geschichte des Altertums* represents; but it must not remain unspoken how narrowly MEYER seems to have everywhere confined himself to the perspective of the pure historian. He lacks the correct perspective when it comes to questions which must be decided from the loftiest cultural-historical standpoint, and for which a mastery of certain scientific concepts is essential,

---

[1] *Geschichte des Altertums*, 2nd ed., II, p. 673.
[2] *Geschichte des Altertums*, 2nd ed., II, pp. 55, 673, 735, 752, 787, 800.

such as racial history in the treatment of the Indo-Germanic problem, where MEYER unfortunately goes so completely astray. To him stands a monument of scripture, which in itself does not even say anything decisive, and which towers above the clearest considerations to which we are compelled by the world of today. When MEYER, at the meeting of the Berlin Anthropological Society on March 20, 1909, once again cited Tocharian as probable evidence of an original Asiatic homeland for the Indo-Germanics in his lecture on "Ancient History and Prehistory," even though I had presented a far better explanation of the Tocharian question in a lecture only a year earlier, which MEYER had attended, a letter of rejection was handed to him by each of the panelists[1]. It requires a peculiar kind of delusion to consider the migration from Central Europe to Central Asia (Turkestan) to be almost impossible, yet to consider the migration in the opposite direction to be very probable. The findings on the Indo-Germanic question obtained through research with a prehistoric foundation — the primary lens through which he should be interpreting my results — MEYER counters these only with his "sober historical consideration." He would have been better off refraining from such value judgments, which can only make an impression on laymen. Insofar as history can come into question here, which of course ceases to be the case in the final analysis, I have fully taken it into consideration. When MEYER persists with such thoroughly ungrounded views on the Indo-Germanic question, it is precisely because large parts of the ancillary sciences that have a say in the decision of this question are completely foreign to him, or he is only insufficiently familiar with them. His verdict depends on an abundance of prejudices which in this case are coupled with rashness, and which as of today, thank God, is only an exception, even among pure historians. None of the stubbornness of his rhetoric can change that.

When MEYER often points out that the immigration of the Greeks to the Balkan Peninsula is archaeologically intangible, the reply must be that of course not all, but only a fraction of the extensive questions that arise when determining the origins of the European races can be answered with the archaeological method. My method was developed on the material from a region — northern Germany and Scandinavia — which has without question yielded such rich finds and such incisive archaeological research of so high a caliber that it is in this

---

[1] "Alte Geschichte und Prähistorie" (Ancient History and Prehistory), *Zeitschrift für Ethnologie* 1909, pp. 283 ff.

respect unlike any other European lands. Countries with inadequate research are not yet ripe enough to yield definitive answers to my questions; so if the answer here is still uncertain, that does not mean a refutation of either my theses or of the reliability of my research results for other regions.

Research in Greece is far from mature, and therefore all of the ethnographic attributions there are still of a highly provisional character. But with which historical science can one intend to claim that his findings have reached a definitive and final conclusion? Only when we have found the richest and most abundant excavation sites from the end of the Neolithic period and from the Early Bronze Age over the whole of northern Greece and the area north of it up to Bosnia, — sites like Dimini and Sesklo —, where finds lead on into the Mycenaean epoch, only then will we be able to provide a clearer view here. Nothing is more certain to me than that we will one day establish the migratory history of the Greeks in an archaeological way and even if the findings may only be more negative. For if the Greeks did not initially move in with large swarms of rapid and sustained reinforcements, but only with a small warrior caste, which was only just strong enough to exercise military rule from fixed points over a densely populated, subjugated country of higher standing in terms of material culture, without themselves having the opportunity to devote themselves to productive activity in crafts and trades, then it would have been impossible for anything to be preserved from their ancestral culture that, while certainly unique, was of lower standing under these new conditions. That ancient, Pre-Greek culture of the Greeks must have disappeared quickly in the new country, because the small, transplanted Greek upper class that brought it with them grew into the new, superior national culture without influencing it in any noticeable way. This was still the case in the early Mycenaean period with the culture of the Achaeans, which was non-Greek Cretan, and only during their later developments in castle building, in their use of garment pins, in their costumes, in their rejection of the Cretan alphabet, and so on, did they begin to testify anew to their Indo-Germanic independence.

How I regard the state of the Greek question is comprehensively dealt with in the last section of my 1908 lecture on the Indo-Germanics, which unfortunately has not yet been printed, although in its most relevant portions I disagree with the views which Georg WILKE presented in his otherwise stellar book about the "Hellenes and Thracians[1]."

I still must address MEYER's proposition: "With the same arguments which are cited for the permanent settlement of the Baltic Sea region by Indo-Germanics, demographic continuity could be proven for pretty much every country on earth." However, that would be easy if, in the manner of the historians, one rashly jotted down a summary of the prehistoric archaeology results from only handbooks, and then from that summary the settlement history of "the Earth" (!) were produced. MEYER just doesn't have any idea about the enormous amount of individual work invested into the archaeological material under consideration, which must first be collected in total, stringently examined and arranged chronologically, divided into large cultural groups, then in turn compared groupwise in a stringent chronological and typological manner before one can even begin to think about extracting any ethnological results.

It was MONTELIUS who, in 1884 in the *Nordisk Tidskrift*, published his treatise "On the Immigration of Our Forefathers to the North[2]," that is, their immigration to Scandinavia as well as Denmark. Famously, and contrary to the hitherto commonplace rash assumptions of population turnovers, this treatise attested to a cultural transformation which had taken place in only one direction, and most crucially, which took place only very gradually, establishing the proposition: "Cultural continuity indicates the permanence of populations." Of course, MONTELIUS only presented this proposition completely bare, without corroborating it by providing detailed settlement statistics for the area in question, arranged according to periods. He had contented himself with the richness of his insider's view of the distribution of cultures within Scandinavia, which he had gained from his consistent and thorough analysis of the entirety of the material from archaeological finds, and which was therefore undoubtedly correct. For such a closed-off, uniform territory as Scandinavia, which due to its northern location as well as due to the lack of easy accessibility was almost completely protected from any major disturbances to its settlements from the

---

[1] Georg WILKE, "Spiralmäanderkeramik und Gefässmalerei, Hellenen und Thraker" (Spiral-Meander Ceramics and the Painting of Vessels, Hellenic and Thracian). Würzburg 1910. = *Darstellungen früh- und vorgeschichtlicher Kultur-, Kunst- und Völkergeschichte* (Representations of Early Historic and Prehistoric Cultural History, Art History and Folk History), edited by Gustaf KOSSINNA. Heft 1. (*Mannusbibliothek*, No. I).

[2] "über die Einwanderung unserer Vorväter in den Norden" (On the Immigration of Our Forefathers to the North), *Deutsch im Archiv für Anthropologie* 1888. Bd. 17, pp. 151–160.

outside, and shortly thereafter for northern Germany as soon as a fixed and continuous settlement had taken hold, — for such regions as these, this type of evidence sufficed.

For an area such as Central Europe, which is so freely open to the influx of foreign settlers from all sides, and which has always housed a large number of very different cultures, MONTELIUS's type of evidence could not suffice. What I had incorporated into prehistoric research had to be added, the scientific settlement study, the written and cartographic expression of the cultures, that is, of the entirety of the rigorously and scientifically-processed archaeological finds, fully mapped out, sorted into the finest divisions of separate time periods that we can possibly achieve, and all with a keen eye for observing any slight shifts in the evolution or development of artifact types. Does MEYER seriously want us to believe that he has conducted such an investigation in some tiny area of Europe, or that he had someone else work there using my method, or that applying my method always establishes continuity? My results in this outline will convince him otherwise, if he can be convinced at all.

We have had to dwell on Eduard MEYER for a long time, as a man who is rightly regarded as a king in the realm of the history of antiquity. Unfortunately, we still must come to terms with the other two previously mentioned scholars, who can only be counted among *dii minorum gentium*, the linguist Otto SCHRADER and the prehistorian Moriz HÖRNES, both talents that do not have their strengths in synthesis, as ROON demands of the historian, but only as compilers. Rigorous analysis is not their specialty.

SCHRADER himself has opposed my equation "culture group = ethnic group" in two sections of his book *Sprachvergleichung Und Urgeschichte*[1] (Comparative Linguistics and Prehistory), where he dealt with my paper "The Indo-Germanic Question Answered Archaeologically." I cannot go into the Indo-Germanic question as such again here; for that I refer to my report on SCHRADER's works[2], as well as to two relevant statements from my grand lecture of 1908[3]. A special rebuttal against SCHRADER rests, as I wish to reveal to this scholar, unprinted in my desk and will be kept ready for printing, should

---

[1] *Sprachvergleichung Und Urgeschichte: Linguistisch-Historische Beiträge Zur Erforschung Des Indogermanischen Altertums* (Comparative Linguistics and Prehistory: Linguistic-Historical Contributions to the Study of Indo-Germanic Antiquity), 3rd ed., I, pp. 118 ff. and II, pp. 472 f.
[2] BUSCHAN's *Zentralblatt für Anthropologie* 1908, pp. 225 ff.
[3] *Mannus* I, pp. 244 f. and *Mannus* II, pp. 81 ff.

SCHRADER force my hand in the future.

SCHRADER arranges his rejection of my equation according to five major points, only two of which come into consideration for us here.

He first contends that the evidence of the correctness of my equation is lacking. To counter that point, after everything that has preceded this, I really hardly have to muster any further remarks. I only emphasize that the sole attempt to present a refutation of my evidence has been Eduard MEYER's, that which has just been discussed, and that this attempt has failed completely.

But SCHRADER then rejects my demonstration of the evidence that the expansion of cultural groups can only occur as a result of population displacements, and he asserts that the impacts of trade or even the complete transference of culture also come into question here. Well, they certainly come into question for those who approach these things as a novice, but not for those who treat these things with the full tool kit of a cultural historian, in other words as both a comprehensively trained archaeologist and as an anthropologist at the same time. The artillery that SCHRADER is deploying against me here was essentially taken from the arsenal of Prague Sanskritist WINTERNITZ, an almost childishly amateurish scholar in archaeological and especially prehistoric matters, who talked himself into a truly amusing fury with his denial of the well-known fact that one of the defining characteristics of the Neolithic cultures is always their peculiar forms of pottery, to the extent that he said believing this fact is "grotesquely comical." However, this fact has recently also imposed itself upon the classical archaeologists in the field of Southern European prehistory as an incontrovertible truth.

In order to support a point of view here, though it is contrary to my habit to argue in a SCHRADER-like way by using the voices of other scholars instead of my own reasoning, I quote here what Adolf MICHAELIS said about the study of pottery: "This almost indestructible pottery offers the surest and most ubiquitous sign of human culture. For the various types of pottery, their evolution in both form and decoration provides the most valuable guide to the knowledge of distant cultural periods and the connections between them; the cultural-historical and ethnological importance of this ancient pottery far exceeds its value to art history in the narrower sense"[1]! And what did H. BULLE, the successful

---

[1] A. MICHAELIS, *Die archäologischen Entdeckungen des 19. Jahrhunderts* (The Archaeological Discoveries of the 19th Century). Leipzig 1906. pp. 200 f.

discoverer of the Orchomenus of the Stone Age and Bronze Age, observe? After pointing out how the archaeological-cultural historian is able to discern the high points and low points of cultural development, the flowering and the decline of entire races from rows of cultural artifacts of an inconspicuous kind, such as garment pins, he then emphasizes in particular the great value of the "pots" for this type of research. "For archaeologists, clay vessels are always the safest guide when tracking down cultural connections."[1]

These voices, which sounded after mine, could already be sufficient proof for SCHRADER that knowledgeable people do not find it at all "grotesquely comical" to use "prehistoric pots, their form and ornamentation as evidence" for cultural and ethnic units. His insipid jest that "pots should be even more fragile than heads" (SCHRADER means "skulls") will only be received by all true experts with a silent shrug of the shoulders. SCHRADER would have spared himself most of his gaffes had he been inclined to delve into the views of those archaeologists who produce settlement studies along the lines of my method instead of confiding in those who understand nothing about such a study, and who therefore don't even want to know anything about it, like Moriz HÖRNES, who was incensed by my thoroughly honest and objective criticism of his talent, or even the clueless WINTERNITZ.

But have I ever just "identified pots with peoples"? Are my conclusions really built on such inadequate foundations? Haven't I always looked at entire cultures in their main area of distribution as well as in their offshoots? In the case of grave finds, this always includes the peculiar burial rite: whether burial mound or flat grave, whether with or without stone protection, stone coffin, and so on, including the characteristic additions of specifically shaped weapons, implements, jewelry, especially amber and shell jewelry, and so on, and yes, usually even the racial affiliation as well. The dedicated researcher of prehistory knows exactly what kind of rich cultural content is being denoted whenever an expert mentions the simple term "Corded Ware," but not the layman.

It is therefore a very sure sign that SCHRADER has no say in these matters, and is much less authorized to debate them, when he broods over the question of whether it might not merely be cultural transmission or perhaps the effects of commerce here. So there was trade not only with specific weapons, implements, jewelry, and pottery, but also at the same time with specific burial

---

[1] Supplement to the Munich *Allgemeinen Zeitung* 1907, No. 1.

rites, and yes, even with specific racial affiliations! For we have long known that the major disparate cultural areas of even Central Europe can also be distinguished by the peculiar anthropological types belonging to their associated ethnic groups. Moreover, since 1908 we have known through the work of SCHLIZ that each of the larger subgroups of the major cultures also has its own particular racial type. So this must be some truly wondrous type of commerce that we are witnessing here!

With the assumption of a far-reaching trade in all of the finer cultural wares, bothersome mischief had been committed in past decades, admittedly even within the circles of prehistorians themselves, until in the discovery of everywhere-existing regional or even more locally-limited distinctive slight departures from the ostensibly everywhere-identical cultural phenomena, even where uniformity prevailed on a large scale, the criterion was found to arrive at the now long-dominant conviction that the principal bulk of the wares of all cultures were definitely of native origin. First and foremost, this is to be applied to ceramics, and indeed without exception, even in regions where the potter's wheel was still absent, and where at the same time the firing of ceramics was so insubstantial that the transport of clay vessels would have been completely impossible. The formerly much-quoted essay by A. GÖTZE on Neolithic trade already requires quite strong corrections in its overall conception, as the author himself might admit today, but especially so in the section on clay vessels, which it would be best to excise completely. Admittedly, trade was already so well developed in Neolithic times that it conveyed land and sea products not only throughout Europe, but also far beyond Europe, but what the nature of this trade was and what kind of things came into question (primarily jewelry), I have demonstrated in a lecture in Hanover in 1909[1].

The third case of cultural diffusion that SCHRADER offers as a possibility, the complete transference of culture, is even less conceivable than cultural diffusion through trade, since it could only be brought about by an enormous increase in both trade and traffic, and that would be hard to imagine without significant intermixtures of peoples taking place, even if it were to happen today. After all, one would not want to throw the great similarity of today's European cultures at me in the Eduard MEYER-like manner, when anyone who has really studied these cultures would immediately recognize the country

---

[1] *Mannus* I. Supplementary Volume. pp. 2 ff. (Brief provisional extract).

they are in just from the external appearance of today's cultural products and cultural forms, without needing a diploma in any written or spoken language. No, such a far-reaching combination of trade and traffic would be enough of an absurdity today, let alone in prehistoric times, but even if we hypothetically consider such cases: for the prehistoric times, for example the Neolithic epoch, we would then be dealing with a diffusion of cultures where in most cases no perceptible trace of variation can be detected.

Admittedly, here SCHRADER also seems to have some better information about prehistory, on par with that of the experts, otherwise he could not claim that archaeology "only determines with some degree of certainty the ethnic foundations of antiquities that are closest to history and, for example, one could speak of Slavic and Celtic finds," to which he elsewhere[1] adds the Frankish finds, though he adds that this is because "in later epochs" a "greater differentiation of cultures" occurs. But what does archaeology have to say about this, for example in Central Europe? The exact opposite! Today's Germany has not had a completely uniform culture for a long time, but the cultural variants in the different areas are all very similar. It was very much the same in the earliest centuries of history, around the time when our calendar begins, although the West Germanic and East Germanic peoples were separated by a cultural boundary that, in my opinion, does not exist with such sharpness today. If we go back further, then in northern Germany alone after half a millennium or so we come to three extremely mutually exclusive cultures, the Germanic, the Celtic, and the Illyrian, each of them with a number of sub-divisions in their individual areas. If we go back even further, to the third to fourth millennium BC, we encounter in Germany such an abundance of largely contemporaneous Neolithic cultures that we have hardly come close to observing the likes of it in previous cases. I shall spare you the rest of the argument against SCHRADER.

SCHRADER is by no means alone in his doubts. Other linguists have also expressed themselves in the same spirit or at least have similar thoughts, likewise so have purely philologically trained researchers of antiquity, both Germanists and classical philologists, and to some extent even prehistorians. Of the latter, this is usually only done by those who do not look outside of some limited boundary, possibly only within their excavation area, or by that class of "researchers" in the mold of Moriz HÖRNES, whose research instinct is fully

---

[1] SCHRADER, *Sprachvergleichung Und Urgeschichte*, 3rd ed., Part I, p. 211; Part II, footnote p. 476.

satisfied once they have described their artifacts more or less intelligibly, or, if the circumstances demand it, their cultural groups, while the quite public secret of my way of doing ethnographic prehistory consists precisely of surveying the entirety of the relevant material and then, under the strictest observation of the chronology of the available finds established through in-depth, specialized research into how the various types of artifacts evolved, to compose a scientific settlement study according to my method.

Anyone who, like me, has been collecting his material for decades and is constantly trying to bring it up to date with the latest scientific developments, as well as constantly checking the cartographic record of this collection and the daily increase of results which flow from it, knows that that he is not striving for yesterday and today, but that his work rests firmly on an indestructible foundation and that he can therefore ignore the amateurish talk of doubt with a smile and a shrug of the shoulders. In this certitude I have for many years ignored the numerous attacks on my work, within which calmness and objectivity are often found in inverse proportion to the prevailing extent of expertise, and I have continued to work in silence for posterity, unconcerned about the present. I thought that if Frederick the Great, as he wrote to Voltaire in 1775, had learned with age "to become a good mail horse, making its way without concern for the yapping of the street dogs," a humble German scholar need not be too distressed when in the end he is denied the respect and recognition to which he feels he is entitled by a number of fellow researchers. However, lately my friends and students have pressed me so strongly that, in the interests of science and of the impact of the "new direction" in prehistory, I have given in to their wish not to ignore these attacks from now on. So it was not out of inclination and personal necessity, but solely out of consideration for a healthier, richer development of both prehistoric archaeology in general and of the particular movement within it which I represent that I have finally been moved to speak up with this brief defense of the method of this science. Unfortunately, there was no way around putting a spotlight upon the major lack of clarity from the opposing camp.

But as far as I can see, I unfortunately haven't yet settled accounts with my third antagonist, Moriz HÖRNES, whom I've mentioned several times.

"Unfortunately," I have to say, because for that we must plunge to a level still far below SCHRADER, almost down to the lowest level of scholarship, to the level of the pure compiler. The treatment of the ethnological findings of prehistoric archaeology has always had an effect on HÖRNES like that of a red rag to a bull. For decades he has been ranting, as if his very existence depended on it, against this kind of prehistoric enterprise. It doesn't suit him at all, he confesses that he doesn't have the slightest talent for it, and yet he feels called upon to let his voice be heard over and over about these things. What he brings forth is not rigorous and objective criticism, which always contains a positive kernel of the advancement of science, but rather exercises in biting mockery and bitter gall, or to put it another way, rhetorical works that only have the purpose of getting something said, rather than to steer us towards the truth and towards the increase of knowledge. Such denigrations are of course often only possible because HÖRNES "misunderstands" much or most of it, and just as obviously and in the most unabashed way distorts a great deal of it, and in doing so he does not shy away from misleading his readers in the worst way. As far as I am concerned, I could just refer to the few lines, or rather the few words, with which I addressed him in passing when I had previously dealt with SCHRADER[1]. To anyone who wants to get a quick idea of the nature of these critical products from the Moriz HÖRNES workshop, I recommend looking at his three reports on the archaeological-ethnological writings of G. WILKE, K. PENKA, and L. PIGORINI, all of which have the same tone, which HÖRNES published together in an issue of the *Zentralblatt für Anthropologie*[2], and then the second extended rehash of his report on WILKE's writing, with which he delighted the *Prähistorische Zeitschrift*, as well as WILKE's "defense" in the same journal[3], which was devastating to HÖRNES, I may add. These five writings are all you need to get to know HÖRNES in all his glory. It is an impotent scolding and rumbling that he offers without making the slightest attempt to create anything like his own scientific thought. This compiler is one of the most thought-poor scholars who holds a university chair in German lands today.

But almost greater than his aversion to ethnological archaeology is his annoyance at the successes that, if pursued in a truly scientific manner, it must bring in, and has already brought in. As he confesses, these laurels keep him up at night, and so he tries his hand here and there, contrary to his most sacred principles, even in this domain, whereby he naturally, in order not to appear too ridiculous, lays his supposed results at the feet of those researchers who are committed to prehistoric ethnology. It is very amusing to see how HÖRNES

---

[1] *Mannus* II, p. 81.
[2] *Zentralblatt für Anthropologie* 1910, pp. 358 ff., p. 362, pp. 371 ff.
[3] *Prähistorische Zeitschrift* 1910, pp. 234 ff.; pp. 422 ff.

squirms in the process; but it is also sad to see how amateurishly he approaches such questions, and how he always strays down the wrong path.

For example, in the treatise in which he has disseminated the raw material he had compiled on the "Hallstatt culture"[1] and presented it to the willing reader for their own intellectual digestion and exploration[2], it says in a footnote (p. 278): "Whoever wants to use names of races and ethnic groups may call the first group (the 'southeastern': in the southern East Alpine countries) Illyrian, the second and fourth (the 'central' in the northern East Alpine countries and the upstream Danube area, and the 'western' in southern and western Germany, northern Switzerland and eastern France) Celtic, the third (the 'northeastern' in the Upper Palatinate, northern Bohemia, northern Moravia, Silesia, and Posen) Germanic; it would not be entirely incorrect." Well, HÖRNES may content himself with that thought; man errs as long as he strives. But no one who has dealt with the ancient history of peoples in Europe — I'm not even talking about the purely prehistoric period — will be able to absorb this ethnological attempt without shaking his head. Namely because two of these four attributions of cultures to specific ethnic groups, the second to the Celts instead of the Northern Illyrians, and the third to the Germanics instead of the Illyrians, are entirely wrong.

In an earlier passage in the same Hallstatt treatise (p. 244), HÖRNES unnecessarily refers to the distribution of House Urns. "To our racial explorers of prehistory," he says, "I recommend accepting that a homogeneous, naturally 'dolichocephalic, Aryan' population of the Bronze Age was broken apart and split in two towards the end of the second millennium BC by the invasion of a naturally 'brachycephalic foreign folk' *(Homo alpinus?)* arriving from the east, who brought with them the knowledge of iron. Should that present them with difficulties, they will also be able to remedy them in their familiar way; — that is not my concern." It is interesting to see that HÖRNES believes that Italy came to the working of iron later than the Alpine countries; but it is even more interesting to see that he hasn't the faintest idea of the scientific principles which one has to observe within prehistoric ethnology. Any quite sporadic cultural phenomenon that appears in two areas that are far apart from each other, and moreover, at very different times, is enough for him to prove ethnic kinship: a truly dilettantish kind of scientific

---

[1] *Archiv für Anthropologie* N. F. III, 1905, pp. 233 f.
[2] Even such an extraordinarily mild critic as A. LISSAUER did not find anything in his review of HÖRNES's treatise with which he could agree, let alone, — which he could praise! *Zeitschrift für Ethnologie* 1905, pp. 787 f.

enterprise, which, despite all of my efforts, will certainly not be eradicated any time soon. Have we not recently seen a new prehistorian making his tribal groupings on the basis of the occurrence of warts, knobs, noses, or humps in the pottery of every period[1]? Science has more to do than to rouse the lovers of such flights of fancy from their smug reverie and stir them to serious work and self-reflection.

One need not interject that HÖRNES only wanted to use the quoted terms to parody the extremely inconvenient direction of today's research into prehistory. That he considers the affirmative content of these sentences to be extremely valuable and at all costs does not want it to be lost to science is shown by the fact that he repeated them in all earnestness and with almost the same wording — dispensing only with his spiteful taunts towards prehistoric ethnology — in his latest compilation, which is called *Natur- und Urgeschichte des Menschen* (Natural History and Prehistory of Man), and which is best distinguished by its particular corpulence (II, p. 83).

* * *

So, we hold steadfastly to the equation "cultural areas are ethnic tribes," and now we will briefly describe how to further our work with this equation.

With the aid of methodical settlement archaeology, we are able to discern how each of the cultural groups representing the respective tribes and ethnic groups of Central Europe expanded and increased in scope or contracted and decreased in scope during the various periods. If precise typological research, by which I mean the developmental and evolutionary history of the various types of implements, weapons, jewelry, burial methods, etc., enlightens us about the connections and contrasts between cultures, a rigorous application of the chronological methods of archaeology — which often must identify the precise century of an artifact or cultural group from within the entirety Metal Age — shows us where a culture found uninterrupted, steady continuity over its entire area or at least in its main area, and where it must have suffered a disruption in settlement. Both of these together: the typological description of a certain cultural group of a certain period in connection with a rigorous chronological investigation of the mother and daughter groups, that is, the cultural phases that preceded and succeeded the primary cultural group being examined: these

---

[1] *Prähistorische Zeitschrift* I, pp. 351 ff.: "Buckelkeramik" (Knobbed Ware).

combined are more than sufficient to yield the fruits of our settlement archaeology. They show how some areas have throughout the millennia been inhabited with more or less uniform density and always by the same major ethnic group, though not always by the same tribe, such as Scandinavia; and in contrast, how in other areas sudden and severe disruptions in settlement, rapid or prolonged emigration, prolonged depopulation, or rapid or prolonged immigration must have been experienced. It is also the case that a culture sprouts younger offshoots not only on its native soil, but at the same time also in distant colonial lands, perhaps separated by an inlet of the sea, whereby under certain circumstances the mother soil becomes uninhabited, as can be observed to have happened repeatedly in the earlier prehistoric times. But just as often, indeed even more often, the culture — that is, the tribal group — that was transplanted colonially sees its uniqueness die out on the new soil, sometimes quickly, sometimes more slowly: it ends up being absorbed into, or, to put it better, replaced by the indigenous cultural and ethnic group that is burgeoning anew, which on its native soil was only able to be temporarily suppressed. That is the fate of all Indo-Germanic tribes overflowing across immeasurable distances, so long as they make their way into a climate that is unsuitable for them and stay there; just as it was with the Germanics of the Völkerwanderung insofar as they advanced southwards beyond Central Europe.

If the troop of emigrants is small or very small relative to the new land it has conquered, especially if that land is densely populated, and perhaps also much more advanced than the conquering troop, then the latter cannot impart its uniqueness upon the further course of cultural development in the new land; rather, it ends up being culturally subjugated by the native class, just as it had subjugated them politically. Only with continuous replenishment from the homeland can the conquering troop then become so strong that they, supported by state-like power and superiority, give the subjugated indigenous majority, now severely culturally-damaged and degenerated by its oppression, a new culture, a culture in which both parts of the population from then on participate, having an equal or unequal share over its influence depending on each of their particular characteristics.

An ethnic migration sometimes takes place so imperceptibly and silently, especially when it rushes across very great distances, that the remnants of the culture of the homeland that can be discovered at the final destination are few or nil. Yet this movement nevertheless betrays itself by the fact that it causes a sudden flow of traffic from the new land in the opposite direction back to the region of the homeland. Such was the case at the beginning of the Bronze Age with Italy and Central Europe; in the early historical times with Gothic-ruled southern Russia and eastern Germany; and in the 17th or 18th centuries with North America and Western and Central Europe.

II.

From these vantage points we will now turn to the origin of the Germanics; of course, we will not arrive at the origin of the Germanic family itself, because we would have to venture abroad to do so, so we must content ourselves with determining the region from which the Germanics came to Germany and the point in time when this happened.

In order to discover the origin of the Germanics, we first must take a close look at the Germanic peoples during the times of the richest and best historical tradition using the previously described method which I have been using for decades. This was undoubtedly the time of the 1st century AD, when Roman sources and Greek sources fed by Roman conveyances flowed abundantly, such that we can identify not just the deeds and the destinies of the individual Germanic tribes with relative clarity, but also their circumstances, their dwellings, and their settlement areas.

With this picture of the map of Germania that we have obtained from literary tradition, be it from around 100 or 200 years after Christ, or from around Christ's birth, I will now compare the picture of the map of this period that is painted for us by the record of all of the countless Germanic archaeological finds from this exact period. The result is a surprising correspondence between the two pictures, with the only difference being that the settlement map obtained by archaeological means is much more precise in the designation of the borders of the cultural areas than the tribal map drafted according to what writers had reported when defining the major ethnic groups. First of all, we see the exact border between the West Germanic and East Germanic peoples, which PTOLEMY had inaccurately fixed to the Oder line around 150 AD, but which according to the archaeology of the local soil, had changed across the centuries in such a way that since its first appearance in the 8th century BC it constantly advanced westward, first only gradually approaching the Oder, and finally pushing across it and onward from there to midway between the Elbe and the Oder.

In the case of the West Germanics, we know from Pliny and Tacitus that the three major tribes were the Ingvaeones by the sea (along the coast of the North Sea and in Denmark), the Istvaeones on the Rhine border from Mainz and on downward and eastward to the Leine River, and finally, in the interior of Germania, the Irminones, or the Suebian groups. The archaeology of the 1st century AD reveals the same great tripartite division. Among the last-mentioned Irminones we find the main mass of the West Germanics: the Elbe Germanics with their Meander Urns, from northern Bohemia down to Hamburg, from Brunswick in the west to Stettin and Frankfurt in the east, and across to the right bank of the Oder. Completely separate from the culture of the Elbe Germanics was the culture of the other two West Germanic tribal groups, on the one hand the tribes in Schleswig-Holstein, Jutland, and also on the Danish islands, which according to archaeological and linguistic evidence were still West Germanic at that time, had a "German-English" population so-to-speak — these are the Ingvaeones. On the other hand, the culture of the Rhine Germanics was just as isolated, but of course we do not yet know enough about them archaeologically, so they differ more negatively than positively from the Elbe Germanics — these are the Istvaeones.

As we progress backwards in time from this picture from the 1st century AD into the previous period, the so-called La Tène archaeological period, which encompassed the last four to five centuries of the era before Christ, the authority of ancient sources begins to abandon us more and more. However, we still know some details from the historical tradition, and we still have some clues from the linguistic field. Of course, research into the names of these ancient cites is an extremely difficult field of study, and the results are by no means as reliable as was once believed. In this period, during the last 150 years before Christ, archaeologically speaking we can very clearly see the traces of a peculiarly Germanic culture, which itself shows strong Celtic influence, extending outwards from Saxony-Thuringia, so from the Saale-Elbe area to Hesse-Nassau and further to Rhine-Hesse[1]. This is the expansion of the Elbe-Suebi to the Lower Main region, where we are greeted by their most far-flung western division in the form of Caesar's Suebi. — We must also recognize the strong and apparently dominant

---

[1] In this whole stretch of land, the Germanics were successors to the Celts, who had only just been ousted from here, and whose cultural influence on the Germanics is archaeologically particularly clear in the ceramics, which exhibit numerous very beautiful, fine-toned, glossy-black, thin-walled, turned clay vessels.

Germanic components of the originally purely Celtic Treveri between the Moselle and the Rhine during the last two centuries before Christ, which Caesar, Strabo, and Tacitus had also mentioned. I have even succeeded in uncovering an in itself tiny but completely clear, undoubtable connection between the settlement of the Suebian king Ariovistus in Lower Alsace around 70 or 60 BC and the simultaneous culture of Suebian Ober-Havelland and Mecklenburg-Strelitz in a grave belonging to the end of the La Tène period near Niedermodern, at the point of intersection of the districts of Saverne, Haguenau, and Strasbourg[1].

We can then, even further back in time, very clearly recognize archaeologically the historically attested conquest and settlement of the northern Gauls across the area north of the Alps around the year 400 BC, namely in Thuringia, the Austrian Sudetenland, and Bohemia and Moravia. The culture that was peculiar to these Gauls including their funerary rite of burial without cremation enabled me to precisely define the southern border of the West Germanic Empire from the Saale to Mainz-and-Koblenz during the early and middle La Tène period, so around 400–150 BC, to be precise.

During that same period, as we venture further back in time, the more we see the frontier of the East Germanics receding further and further to the east, thus their territory is shrinking more and more, especially during the time of the Face Urn culture on the Vistula and the Upper Oder. We can see the beginnings of this culture emerging on the west bank of the lower Vistula at the dawn of the Iron Age around the 8th century BC, or about 700 BC.

But this is precisely the easternmost point to which, during the immediately-preceding period, the fifth and final period of the Bronze Age, so around 900–700 BC, the culture of the West Germanics had advanced from the west, from the lower Oder, and onwards through Eastern Pomerania. In a countercurrent to this West Germanic wave, the culture of the East Germanics, which was itself first taking shape around 700 BC, advanced westward from Danzig across a large part of Eastern Pomerania, following on the heels of the border of the West Germanics, which was now retreating again. It also advanced southwards through Bromberg, then from Posen to northern Silesia, driving out a third culture and ethnic group in front of it which had existed there much earlier, in the middle-to-early Bronze Age, in Period III, Period II, and even already in Period I, that is, before 2000 BC, when it had taken possession of the

---

[1] *Korrespondenzblatt der Deutschen anthropologischen Gesellschaft* 1907, pp. 59 ff.

same area, Silesia, Posen, Lusatia, Neumark, the Kingdom of Saxony, southern Brandenburg, and also reaching further westward into the country up to the Saale. This non-Germanic ethnic tribe with a culture that was completely different from the Germanic ones had immigrated northwards from Silesia, Bohemia, Moravia, and western Hungary — where it had developed from the even older population of the closing segment of the Stone Age — and settled in eastern Germany as the southeastern neighbors of the Germanics in an area which in even earlier times, that is, before 1500 BC, had been uninhabited for a long time. This is the ethnic group that I call the Illyrians.

So clearly for the East Germanics it was relatively late, only at the beginning of the Iron Age, that we recognize a first dawn of culture and an original founding settlement at the mouth of the Vistula — alone from which we must necessarily deduce an overseas origin for these tribes, namely that of southern Scandinavia. Just as clearly, the opposite behavior can be observed for the entire large West Germanic settlement area in northern Germany: namely, a seamless connection going back almost to the beginning of the Bronze Age, without a discontinuity in culture, without a discontinuity in settlement. Nevertheless, this territory from Angermünde, passing through Prenzlau to Friedland in Mecklenburg-Strelitz, and then from there up to the mouth of the Peene near Wolgast had also narrowed somewhat in the earlier periods of the Bronze Age, particularly in the east, where during the second period of the Bronze Age (1700 to 1400 BC) the eastern border of the Germanics had retreated to the valley of the lowest reaches of the Oder near the Brandenburg-Pomeranian border, so roughly from Schwedt on the Oder and on downstream from there. The East Germanics did not yet exist during that time.

The continuation of this borderline stretched from Angermünde, through Eberswalde, and on to Berlin, where it met the southern boundary of the Germanics, this borderline then stretched out westwards in an inwardly-curved line towards the river Elbe, which it reached at the mouth of the Saale near the town of Kalbe, and then continued a little further upstream to Bernburg before veering directly westward to Quedlinburg and Blankenburg; both towns which still exhibited a culture that was clearly recognizably Germanic, while the neighboring towns of Thale and Ballenstedt contained grave sites that were just as recognizably Celtic around this time. This borderline continued along the northern foot of the German Central Uplands, along the Harz, the Hildesheim Hills, the Deister, the Bückebergen, the Wiehen Hills, and the northwestern corner of the Teutoburg Forest to the Ems, where it then formed the western border as it ran downriver to the sea.

The land area enclosed between this border and the coastline of the sea was at that time a highly suitable place to serve as a cradle and site of cultivation for a united, singular people who resembled nobody other than themselves, just as the Germanics still remained in the time of Tacitus. For its inhabitants were protected from any exceptionally close contact with foreign peoples that would disturb their peculiarity, in the eastern part of this region this protection was provided by wide desolate areas, and in the western part by uninterrupted, very broad mountain ranges, and all the more so by the fact that everywhere along the border of this region the settlements became very thin, most of all towards the west, as it is there on the Ems that we finally completely lose all traces of any of their settlements from this period.

But things didn't remain that way in the west either; here, too, we can archaeologically trace a gradual filling in of the sparsely populated borderlands, and finally an advance of the Germanic frontiers; thus, during the fifth period of the Bronze Age (1000–750 BC), the Ems was crossed and the middle and upper Lippe area was occupied around the central hubs of Haltern and Paderborn; likewise, the Teutoburg Forest was settled at this time, as was the Weser Valley on upward to Höxter. In the Early Iron Age, the Germanics took possession of the Lower Rhine, and in the last centuries before the birth of Christ, the conditions on the western border developed in such a way that the entire Rhine area, including the stretches on the left bank of the Rhine, were in the hands of the Germanics, for whom only Caesar was able set a boundary at the Rhine, although of course he was only able to set it as a political boundary. He could only prevent new incursions by the Germanics on the right bank of the Rhine into areas on the left bank of the Rhine; he could only sever the settled Germanic upper class on the left bank of the Rhine from the main body of their people by establishing this Rhine border, which thereby led to their rapid Celticization.

However, the people from whom the Germanics of northwestern Germany had wrested their new territory at the conclusion of the Bronze Age and during the Early Iron Age up to the time of Caesar were the Celts, whose original homeland was Bohemia and who at the end of the Early Bronze Age, the end of Period I — I call this phase Ic — left Bohemia along the same path that the Bavarians took two millennia later when they first united as an ethnic tribe, the path to the upper Danube. Here, from the foot of the Alps during the second period of the Bronze Age, with a singular, homogeneous culture which sharply contrasted with those of the Germanics, the Celts had spread out across southern Germany, including northern Switzerland and the neighboring eastern France, and on northwards up to the Teutoburg Forest, the Weser Uplands, and the Harz.

If we now go back even further with the Germanics, back into the period of the Early Bronze Age, Period I, the settlement conditions become far more complicated. Within this period, as within the second period, I can distinguish three distinct phases, which I trace backwards in time from about 1700 BC to the 3rd millennium. I now observe how in the second period of the Bronze Age (1700–1400) the Germanic area between the Elbe and the Weser was quite heavily populated, while to the east of the Elbe in Mecklenburg, Western Pomerania, and northern Brandenburg it was far less populated.

If we go even further back to the third and final phase of the Early Bronze Age, Period Ic (2000–1750), we see that the disparate behavior of the two Germanic areas in northern Germany that were separated by the Elbe became yet more pronounced, such that the amount of settlement to the east of the Elbe was almost nil, while to the west of the Elbe, while there seems to have been less than in Period II, the amount of settlement was still considerable.

Yet further back, in the last centuries of the 3rd millennium (before 2000 BC), we see a complete reversal of these settlement conditions. The areas of northwestern Germany between the Leine and the Rhine on the one end, and between the North Sea and the southern German Danube on the other, had back then been unpopulated for a long series of centuries. Conversely, eastern Germany, including the western banks of the Elbe and Thuringia, was back then quite heavily populated.

We must then ask ourselves the question: How can these complete gaps in settlement be explained? We can only explain these phenomena if we journey back beyond these gaps into the preceding period of settlement, which takes us to the closing of the Neolithic epoch, that is, the end of the Stone Age. The culture then dominant in northwestern Germany, characterized among other things by burial mounds which contain peculiar cambered, tall, and slender ceramic beakers, which are called "Zoned Beakers" after their ornamental patterns divided into zones, manifests itself quite similarly England and Scotland, whitherto it must have been transmitted from northwestern Germany by a migratory population influx[1]. Germanics in the true sense of the term can hardly have been the bearers of this movement, especially since this culture of northwestern Germany had no equivalents in the lands east of the Elbe. Rather, we are dealing with a segment of the Northern Indo-Germanics within northern Germany at this time which had severed every connection with the Germanic Northern Indo-Germanics, and from whom not even a drop of blood could still live on in the later Germanics[2]. We must state the same for eastern Germany, with the only difference being that the large gap there did not yet arise at the very beginning of the Bronze Age, but only appeared during the middle and end of the early period, during phases Ib and Ic, while during Period Ia of the Bronze Age there was still a full, uninterrupted continuation of culture bridging back to the preceding Neolithic culture of eastern Germany.

Our view of the importance of the large settlement gaps in Period I of the Bronze Age is fully secured when we consider that the early Period Ia as we saw represented in eastern Germany, which was marked by depopulation in northwestern Germany, was also absent in Scandinavia, but by no means due to depopulation; rather, this cultural period was represented here by another one that presented itself as a longer fading-out of the Stone Age culture, only colored by certain influences from the Bronze culture of eastern Germany from Period Ia, which therefore means there was no population gap at all for Scandinavia. In Scandinavia, the full Early Bronze culture only begins with Period Ic, and this is also the same period that the Bronze culture first appeared in northwestern Germany between the Elbe and Rhine, because previously there had been a gap in settlement, while this cultural period (Ic) was almost completely absent in eastern Germany, because a gap in settlement now appears there during this time. Moreover, the unique cultural forms, types of implements, and so on from Period Ic in both northwestern Germany and Scandinavia also correspond quite strikingly.

---

[1] These slender "Zoned Beakers" must not be confused with the short and wide "Bell Beakers," as still commonly happens now, especially by MONTELIUS and Soph. MÜLLER; compare *Mannus* I, p. 232 along with Table XXII; p. 267, footnote p. 272; *Mannus* II, footnote p. 178.

[2] In addition to the Germanics, I count the Celts, Illyrians, Greeks, and Italics among the Northern Indo-Germanic peoples, that is, the Indo-Germanic peoples grouped together as a centum group by linguistic research, while the Southern Indo-Germanic peoples of the Danube region, who coincide with the satem group of linguistic research, are made up of the Thracians, Slavo-Letts, and Indo-Iranians (see *Mannus* I, pp. 21 ff.).

So, to summarize briefly: in northern Germany the Bronze culture appeared as early as Period Ia, but in Scandinavia only during Ic, because the Stone Age still prevailed there during Ia and Ib. Bronze culture Ia and Ib can only be found in northeastern Germany, and not in northwestern Germany, because back then there was instead a gap in settlement there. Conversely, during Ic there was a settlement gap in northeastern Germany; while in northwestern Germany the Scandinavian form of the Early Bronze Age culture increasingly began to appear then, but not the Swiss-South German form or the Hungarian-Austrian form, which both differed so greatly.

Our conclusion is therefore a completely safe one: During Period Ic, the Germanics from Schleswig-Holstein and Jutland, and perhaps also from the Danish islands and Scania, immigrated westwards across the Elbe to a henceforth wholly culturally congruent northwestern Germany. So, if we exclude Schleswig-Holstein, these were the first Germanics in Germany.

Those populations that lived in northern Germany before that, that is, the people of Period Ia of the Bronze Age who lived in the lands east of the Elbe, as well as the entire population of northern Germany during the Neolithic period, are neither Germanics nor their forefathers, but rather they are those tribes of the Northern Indo-Germanics who — insofar as they did not perish before they became known to history — became the other ethnic groups of the Northern Indo-Germanic family who, partly in Central Europe and partly in Southern and Southeastern Europe, gained great names for themselves; such as the Celts throughout western and southwestern Germany, the Illyrians south of the middle Danube, and the Greeks and Italics in their well-known seats of power (see p. 29).

Of interest to and most closely interrelated with this discussion is the fact that the river which in its lowest reaches forms the oldest southern border of the actual Germanic tribes, the Lower Elbe in Holstein from Lauenburg to Cuxhaven, bears a name that came from the original Scandinavian homeland of the Germanics where it serves as a permanent designation for stretches of river both large and small: Göta elv, Ångerman elv, and so on, and *elv* had undoubtedly already served as such a designation in the Stone Age, even if the names which distinguish them, such as Göta elv's name based on that of the surrounding ethnic tribe, may have originated much later. The Indo-Germanic tribes from the middle reaches of the Elbe, so roughly from Lauenburg upwards to the Saale tributary near Barby, as well as the very uniform tribes of the Elbe's upper reaches from Barby to northern Bohemia may have given the river a completely different name in the Neolithic and the Early Bronze Age. But since their advance to the south, the Germanics have in any case enforced the Germanic name that they used for this river along the entire course of the Elbe, even before the arrival of the historical tradition.

III.

Once we see the gaps in population which appeared and disappeared in opposite directions in the two main areas of northern Germany during the Early Bronze Age being filled again as we journey further backwards in time to the end of the Stone Age, we no longer see one uniform culture covering the entirety of Scandinavia and northern Germany, but there is still a coherent cultural group by the North and Baltic Seas composed of different shades of one and the same basic culture, the southern members of which can be traced back to the cultures of central Germany, which were somewhat divergent but which still emerged from the same foundational origins. This entire Neolithic population mass from Scandinavia to Bohemia, Thuringia, and Hesse could be understood in a certain sense as "Germanics," since they are undoubtedly culturally as well as anthropologically, that is, in terms of blood, of one and the same tribe. Nevertheless, they can only be described as Northern Indo-Germanics, since the proportion of this mass that was by far the largest in terms of population, the ones that resided in Germany, gradually separated themselves geographically and largely left Central Europe forever, some as early as the Stone Age and others only in the Early Bronze Age. We can therefore no longer refer to these limbs that were severed from the greater Germanic body as Germanics, much as the Germanic tribes that left Germany during the second great bloodletting of the Germanic body, the Germanic Völkerwanderung at the end of the age of the Roman Empire, which in foreign lands suffered a complete fusion with alien subpopulations, are no longer entitled to be called "German," which would not change even in the case we well know did not occur in which these lost limbs of Germany had not abandoned their ancestral language, but had retained the vigor to continue to develop it organically, that is, completely independently (see the table on p. 29).

Even for the part of the whole body being discussed that can undoubtedly be called purely Germanic, that is, the Scandinavian population, who by blood are the direct ancestors of the Germanics of northern Germany, and thus also of us Germans today, the Stone Age in a certain sense means the Indo-Germanic Epoch, or at least the Northern Indo-Germanic Epoch of their existence, insofar as the epoch of the unified Proto-Indo-Germanic people is archaeologically just as obscure as it has always been linguistically, at least to the critical eye.

Karl MÜLLENHOFF famously considered the point in time when the Germanic language separated from the Proto-Indo-Germanic language, or more precisely, the time when the so-called Germanic sound shift occurred, to be the hour of birth of the Proto-Germanic people. We have long known that towards the end of the Germanic Bronze Age — so around 900 or 1000 BC — the Proto-Germanic language already demonstrated the peculiar Germanic sound pattern, the pattern of the Germanic consonants, which distinguished it from the other Indo-Germanic languages[1]. If we now consider the extent of the Germanic territory during the Early Bronze Age, we see that it stretched from the Swedish province of Medelpad and from Vasa and Helsinki in Finland all the way to Meppen on the Ems, and from Trondheim all the way to Halberstadt and Prenzlau in the Uckermark. The wide distribution of the Germanics across this immensely vast reach of territory necessarily leads to the conclusion that, since such beginnings preordained and guaranteed a fixed direction of consistent, similar further development, the Germanic sound shift had already taken place by the end of the Scandinavian Stone Age[2].

Even this point in time, the end of the Stone Age, would hardly be the one which I would envision as the time of the origin of the Germanics as a distinct ethnic group within the Northern Indo-Germanic family. An undisturbed continuity of cultural development in Scandinavia as well as in northern Germany stretches backwards from the end of the Stone Age around 2000 BC to the beginning of the construction of megalithic tombs around 4000 BC, and from there back somewhat further to form a cultural stage which, even aside from tombs, marks a period of cultural transition from the entire epoch of the later

---

[1] R. MUCH: *Korrespondenzblatt der Deutschen anthropologischen Gesellschaft* 1904, pp. 137 f.

[2] One needn't agonize over this question if he does not consider the Germanic sound pattern, which, according to the current view of linguistic research, must have been very close to the common Proto-Indo-Germanic language, to be a further transformation of the sound patterns of the original language which the remaining Indo-Germanic dialects retained more faithfully, so long as one, along with SCHIRMEISEN (*Mannus, Zeitschrift für Vorgeschichte*, Bd. III. pp. 91 ff.) conversely recognizes consistently more far-reaching degenerations of the root language in these other dialects of Indo-Germanic, which are caused by the emigration and expansion of the bearers of these dialects over ever-greater distances, and by their increased mixing with completely racially-foreign and linguistically-foreign tribes, while at the same time the domestically-remaining Germanic had remained essentially unchanged.

1. Northern Germany excluding Schleswig-Holstein.

Period	Years Before Christ	Between the Ems and Elbe	Between the Elbe and Oder	Between the Oder and Vistula
Late La Tène	Around Christ's birth to 120 BC	Ingvaeones / Istvaeones	Irminones	East Germanics (Vandals, Rugii, Burgundians, and towards the end, Goths)
Middle and Early La Tène	120 — 500	Ingvaeones / Istvaeones	Irminones (also in Altmark and East Hanover)	East Germanics (Vandals)
Earliest Iron Age	500 — 750	West Germanics	Irminones (also in Altmark and East Hanover)	North: East Germanics; South: Northern Illyrians
Bronze Age V	750 — 1050	West Germanics	North: West Germanics; South: Northern Illyrians	North: Distinct eastern group of the West Germanics (Beginning of the East Germanics) South: Northern Illyrians
Bronze Age IV b — III a	1050 — 1400	Germanics	North: Germanics; South: Northern Illyrians	Northwest: Germanics; Northeast and south: N. Illyrians
Bronze Age II c — a	1400 — 1750	Germanics	Northwest: Germanics; Northeast: Northern Illyrians; South: settlement gap	Northern Illyrians
Bronze Age I c	1750 — 1900	Germanics (thin settlement)	Northwest: Germanics; Northeast: Northern Illyrians; South: settlement gap	Northern Illyrians
Bronze Age I b, a	1900 — 2200	settlement gap	North: Germanics and Northern Illyrians; South: settlement gap	Northern Illyrians
Later Stone Age transitional period	2200 — 2400	Northern Indo-Germanics (thin settlement)	Beginning of the Germanics Beginning of the Northern Illyrians	

2. Northern Europe.

Period	Years Before Christ	Schleswig-Holstein, Jutland	Danish Islands	Southern Scandinavia up to Lake Malar	Northern Scandinavia
Early Iron Age	Around Christ's birth to 750 BC	Ingvaeones	Funen: Ingvaeones; Zealand: North Germanics	North Germanics	Proto-Lapps Proto-Finns
Bronze Age V — I c	750 — 1900	Germanics	Germanics	Germanics	Pre-Finns
a) Neolithic Stone Cists; b) Single Earth Graves	1900 — 2400	Beginning of the Germanics (Amalgamation of Northern Indo-Germanics and Finno-Indo-Germanics)			Pre-Finns
a) Later Passage Graves; b) Single Earth Graves	2400 — 2800 (?)	a) East coast and north: Northern Indo-Germanics; b) Inland and west coast: Finno-Indo-Germanics	Northern Indo-Germanics (only sporadically: Finno-Indo-Germanics)	a) West coast: Northern Indo-Germanics; b) East coast: Finno-Indo-Germanics (Boat Axe culture)	Pre-Finns (later "Arctic" civilization)
a) Earlier Passage Graves; b) Single Earth Graves	2800 — 3200 (?)	a) East coast and north: Northern Indo-Germanics; b) Inland and west coast: Finno-Indo-Germanics	Northern Indo-Germanics	a) West coast: Northern Indo-Germanics; b) East coast: Pre-Finns (Dwelling-place culture)	vacant
a) Dolmen; b) Single Earth Graves	3200 — 4000 (?)	a) East coast: Northern Indo-Germanics; b) Inland: Finno-Indo-Germanics	Northern Indo-Germanics	a) West coast: Northern Indo-Germanics; b) East and south coasts: Pre-Finns (later Round-Butted Axes)	vacant
Later Shell Heap (Point-Butted Axes)	4000 — 4500 (?)	a) Proto-Indo-Germanics b) Post-Ice-Age proto-folk	a) Proto-Indo-Germanics b) Post-Ice-Age proto-folk	a) Scania: Proto-Indo-Germanics; b) North and central: Proto-folk (middle Round-Butted Axes)	vacant
Earlier Shell Heap	4500 — 6000 (?)	Pre-Indo-Germanics and Post-Ice-Age proto-folk		a) South: Pre-Indo-Germanics; b) North and central: Post-Ice-Age proto-folk (Nöstvet-Lihult-Round-Butted-Axes-Civilization)	vacant
Ancylus stage	6000 — 10000	Post-Ice-Age proto-folk		South: Post-Ice-Age proto-folk	still glaciated
Yoldia stage	10000 — 15000				still partially glaciated

Neolithic, the epoch of the large tombs, back into the epoch of the earlier Neolithic, which begins with the shell heaps of the Baltic Sea region, and which belongs to cultural stages which date back even further. In this entire period of the later Neolithic, including the aforementioned transitional stage, the Nordic culture, or shall we say the Northern Indo-Germanic culture, had already spread over such large areas of Scandinavia and northern Germany that we undoubtedly can already see divisions into groups and tribes. We can see this most clearly in the time of the megalithic tombs, where Scandinavia and northern Germany, despite all of the great similarities between the cultures, already show very clear differences in grave construction, as well as in the forms of grave goods. So it is here that we already have the full right to speak of the Germanics in Scandinavia, while to the contemporaneous and culturally closely-related, but subsequently-emigrating populations of northern and central Germany we will still have to apply the generic name of the Northern Indo-Germanics.

We are thus observing the same cultural phenomenon with the origin of the Germanics as we did with the origin and the first divisions of the Indo-Germanics, namely that long before linguistics was able to establish the linguistic distance between the languages of certain ethnic groups, archaeology was able to establish the actual geographical and cultural distances between those same ethnic groups. Even during the so-called Copper Age, linguistic unity still existed between all Indo-Germanic tribes; or at least the longest-standing and primary characteristic that is used to mark the first division of Proto-Indo-Germanic peoples into two separate families, the disintegration that led to the distinction between the centum and satem languages, had not yet occurred during that time. In other words, the geographic and cultural separation that had led to sub-divisions within a larger group only much later resulted in a divergence in forms of speech.

Such was also the case with Germanic. The Germanic group as such can be detected at least as far back as the beginning of megalith construction, perhaps even as far back as the previously mentioned transitional epoch; however, we hardly need to trace the inception of the Germanic sound shift, and thus the origin of the Germanic language, back much further than the period of the passage graves (3000 BC).

But the undisturbed continuity in cultural development and especially the continuity of settlement in the region on the coasts of the Baltic Sea and North Sea goes back even further than the previously mentioned transitional epoch to the epoch of the earliest shell heaps in the southwestern Baltic Sea region, the beginnings of which are more likely to be fixed to about 8000 BC rather than to about 7000 BC. On this point of the attribution of the Shell Heap Culture to the Northern Indo-Germanics or simply to Indo-Germanics, I revert to an earlier view of mine, which I unfortunately had abandoned in my most recently published statement[1] on these questions in favor of the dissenting opinion of MONTELIUS, A. M. HANSEN, and others. With the culture of the earliest shell heaps we are obviously witnessing an epoch in which there was no separate Germanic family, but during which the entirety of the Northern Indo-Germanic group was enclosed within a relatively narrow area, which lay almost exclusively on what would later, during the Later Neolithic period, become the purely Germanic soil of southern Scandinavia, Denmark, and Schleswig-Holstein.

On the other hand, even further back during the transition to the cultural epoch of the so-called Ancylus stage of the Baltic Sea (around 8000 BC), we encounter a clear disruption in the continuity of culture, settlement area, and race. The question of the immigration of the Northern Indo-Germanic group into the Baltic Sea region at the onset of the earliest shell heaps thus inevitably arises. Answering it would take us further into Western Europe and into the Paleolithic age and would have to be carried out on an archaeological as well as on an anthropological basis, as I have demonstrated in meticulous detail in the above-cited *Mannus* treatise[2].

---

[1] *Mannus*, Bd. I. 1909. pp. 30 ff.

[2] This treatise should be supplemented on the question of the derivation of the Northern European racial type according to the remarks that I have dedicated to the "Homo Aurignacensis Hauseri" (*Mannus* II, pp. 169 f.); a transformation is due in the conception of the Arctic Stone Age culture, which according to the latest Norwegian research, published shortly after my lecture, can no longer be regarded as a continuation of the Nøstvet culture, which also sees its connection with the Shell Heap Culture broken, but its derivation from the culture of the Ancylus period is untouched. Along with the Shell Heap Culture, the similar Nøstvet culture of southeastern Norway must also be described as Northern Indo-Germanic, while the culture of the Ancylus period, like the Arctic culture which I continue to derive from it, which had its home mainly in both the southeastern and eastern parts of the Baltic Sea region, can be assigned to the Proto-Finns.

SUPPLEMENTS

On Pages 24 and 25 in general: The population of eastern Germany from the end of the Stone Age developed within Period I into the so-called Aunjetitz population (see *Mannus* Bd. 11/12, p. 232), as attested to in its southerly section by graves and archaeological finds, and in the more northerly section exclusively by archaeological finds. These are the beginnings of the Illyrians. The density of their settlements in the northern areas didn't begin to intensify until Period II of the Bronze Age.

On Page 26: In regard to the origin of the Germanics from the amalgamation of the Finno-Indo-Germanics with the Northern Indo-Germanics during the last centuries of the 3rd millennium BC, this can now be compared to my lecture: "Höhepunkte nordindogermanischer Kultur" (High Points of Northern Indo-Germanic Culture) (*Mannus* 11/12, p. 274).

On Pages 28 and 30: My current understanding of the beginnings of the Northern Indo-Germanics within the time and culture of the Dolmen population, the origin of the Indo-Germanics in general at the end of the Shell Heap period (the early stage of which can be attributed to the "Pre-Indo-Germanics" while the even earlier population of the Ancylus and Yoldia stages is to be regarded as a common source for Pre-Indo-Germanics and Pre-Finns) has been alluded to in the cited lecture (*Mannus* Bd. 11/12, pp. 249 ff.) and in a special outline (*Indogermanische Forschungen* Bd. 39, 1920).

CHANGES

Page 13 line 14 from the bottom (including footnotes), page 16 line 18 from the top, page 22 line 9 from the top originally read: Carpo-Dacian, Carpo-Dacians (instead of Illyrian, Illyrians).

Page 21 line 3 from the bottom originally read: in Period III and even at the end of Period II, that is, around 1500 BC.

Page 22 line 4 from the top originally read: had immigrated from the southeast, from Hungary [also did not previously mention the Stone Age population from which they had originated].

Page 22 line 9 from the top (pertaining to the group that Kossinna had formerly called the Carpo-Dacians, and the only line to be removed from this edition) originally read: who are from the northernmost branch of the greater family of the Thracians.

Page 22 line 18 from the top: [The lines describing the extent of this territory were newly added to this edition.]

Page 22 line 11 from the bottom originally read: Schwedt on the Oder (instead of Angermünde).

Page 23 line 17 from the top originally read: 900–700.

Page 24 line 14 from the top originally read: 1800–1700.

Page 24 line 16 from the bottom originally read: In the 2nd and 1st phases of this early period.

Page 28 line 13 from the top originally read: Stargard in Pomerania (instead of: Prenzlau in the Uckermark).

TRANSLATOR'S NOTE

As Kossinna mentioned in the forward, this edition features a significantly reworked table on page 29, and the changes to the table provide great insight into how Kossinna's understanding had evolved over the course of the intervening decade. For one, its original structure was different; instead of Northern Germany excluding Schleswig-Holstein, the top section focused on Northern Germany excluding Thuringia, and rather than dividing that section according to areas between rivers, the subsections were instead a northwestern area, the Elbe area, and a northeastern area. The bottom section of the table only focused on Scandinavia, and with much less detail, with the only subsections being for southern and northern Scandinavia. In that latter section, instead of labeling the population of the Yoldia and Ancylus stages the Post-Ice-Age proto-folk (*nacheiszeitliches Urvolk*), Kossinna simply labeled this population as "not Indo-Germanics," and an arrow indicated that he saw this population moving to Northern Scandinavia to become the Proto-Finns. Consistent with what is said on page 31, he originally marked the arrival of the early Shell Heap Culture around 8000 BC, and he already labeled this population as Northern Indo-Germanics, whereas in this edition's newer table, and as discussed in the last of the supplements on the previous page, he refers to this population as Pre-Indo-Germanics and marks their arrival around 6000 BC. As Kossinna mentions in that last supplement, he now sees the Post-Ice-Age proto-folk as a common source for both the Pre-Indo-Germanics and the Pre-Finns (who, as the name indicates, he views as distinct from the later Proto-Finns). He then at 5000 BC already marked the origin of the Germanics in southern Scandinavia during the later Shell Heap period, whereas here he not only dates that period differently, but now sees that as the time of the formation of the Proto-Indo-Germanics, with the Germanics only forming much later out of an amalgamation of the Northern Indo-Germanics and a group he calls the Finno-Indo-Germanics, the latter of whom he implicitly views as having been derived from a mixture of Pre-Finns and Northern Indo-Germanics. Additionally, rather than identifying the round-butted axes (*Walzenbeil*) as having been present during the earlier Shell Heap period, he previously identified them as only having been present during the later Shell Heap period, together with point-butted axes (*spitznackiges Beil*).

As for the top section, it was also much less detailed, but there are some differences worth mentioning. He had previously indicated that during the transitional period of the Later Stone Age (originally described as the closing of the Neolithic, 2500–2200 BC) the northwestern group of Northern Indo-Germanics migrated to England and Scotland, as mentioned in the footnote on page 24 where he discusses the "Zoned Beaker" culture; that reference was left out here. During the same later Stone Age period, instead of indicating the arrival of the Germanics in the Elbe area and the arrival of the Northern Illyrians in both the Elbe area and the northeastern area, as he does in this edition, he simply indicated that Northern Indo-Germanics were present in these areas. Interestingly, he also noted that this group of Northern Indo-Germanics "will probably become Greeks." As for the Northern Illyrians, they were not mentioned on the original table, as he had called that population the Carpo-Dacians. He previously indicated that this culture had arrived in the northeast around 1500 BC, while here he sees the Northern Illyrians as having arrived much earlier.

Otherwise, the only other significant difference between the two versions of the table is that the chronology of the periods is somewhat different, and the newer version of the table also breaks up the periods into somewhat smaller segments of time. The pages to follow feature the nine maps included with this 1920 edition. The final map on page 43 was included with some earlier copies of the book, but it had originally referred to the Carpo-Dacians rather than the Northern Illyrians. Kossinna's identification of this culture with the Northern Illyrians would go on to become influential in the early-to-mid 20th century, contributing to what were known as Pan-Illyrian theories among German prehistorians and linguists.

Settlement areas of the East Germanics in the Early Iron Age (750—1 BC).

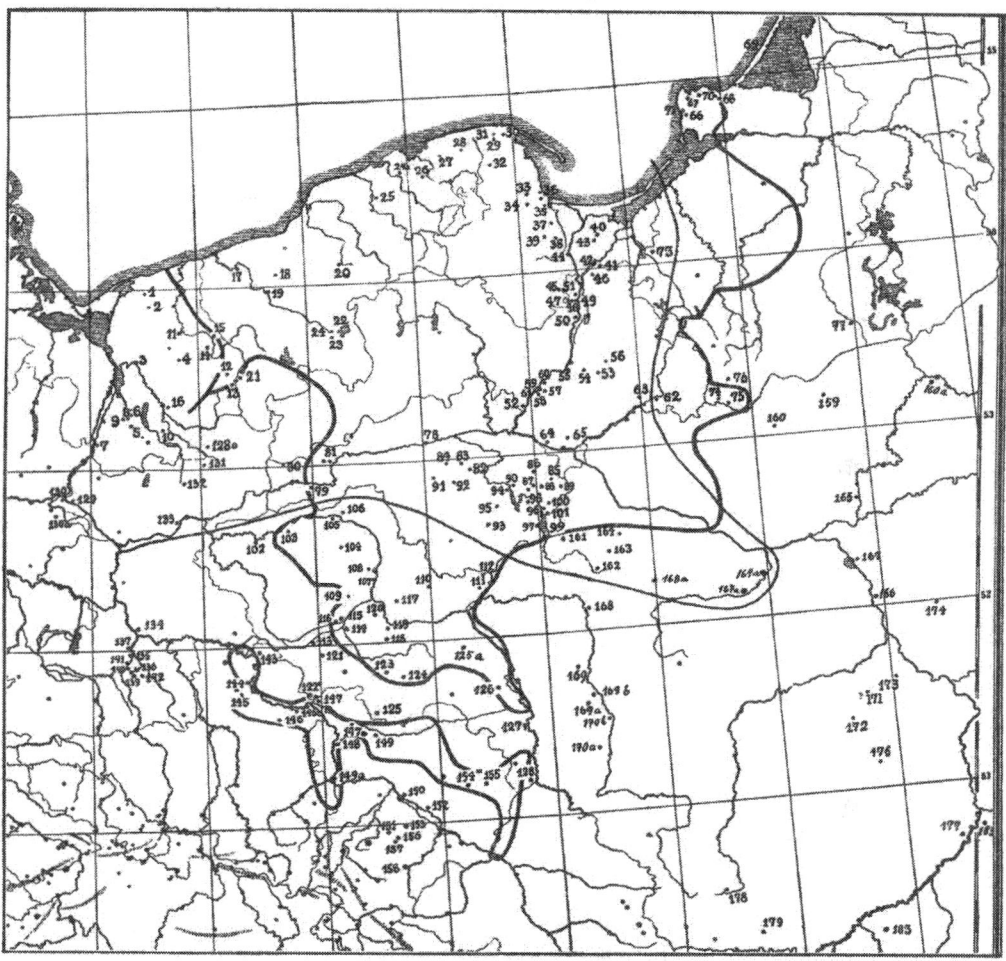

The numbers denote settlement sites of the East Germanics during the late La Tène period: 120—1 BC (per J. Kostrzewski.)

The thinner line, starting from the confluence of the Warthe and the Oder (at No. 135) and ending at the Vistula Spit (at No. 73), marks the presumed boundary between the Burgundian-Rugian (northern) cultural area and the Vandalian (southern and eastern) cultural area inside of the late La Tène period. (per Kostrzewski.)

The thicker line, starting from the mouth of the Rega in Eastern Pomerania (at No. 1) and ending at the northern coast of the Samland peninsula (at No. 70), marks the boundaries of the East Germanic Stone Cists and Face Urns cultural area of the Early Iron Age. A small, separate southern part of this cultural area lies in northern Silesia between No. 143 and 155/123. (per G. Kossinna.)

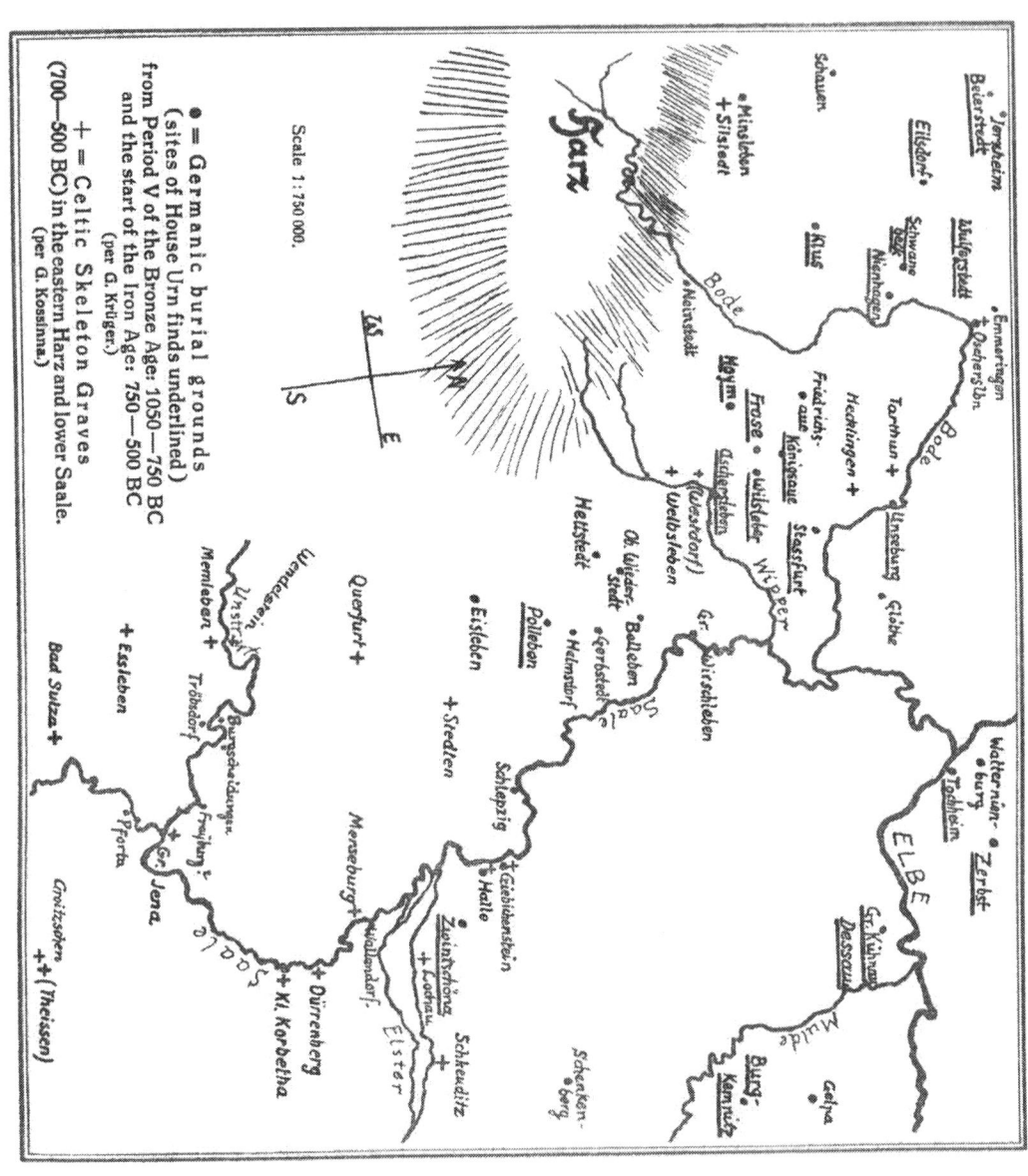

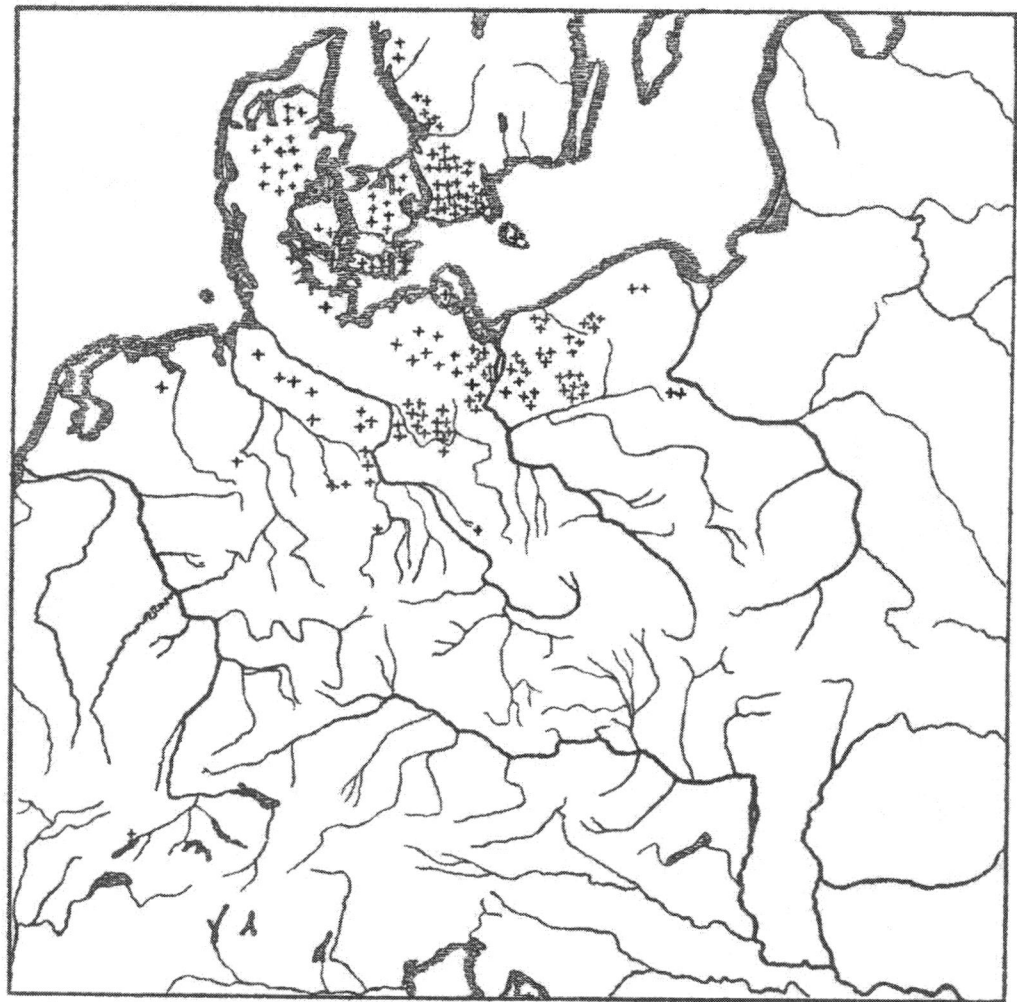

+ = Arched Plate Fibulae (Gewölbte Plattenfibel) from Period V of the Bronze Age (1050—750 BC) as a hallmark of Germanic settlement

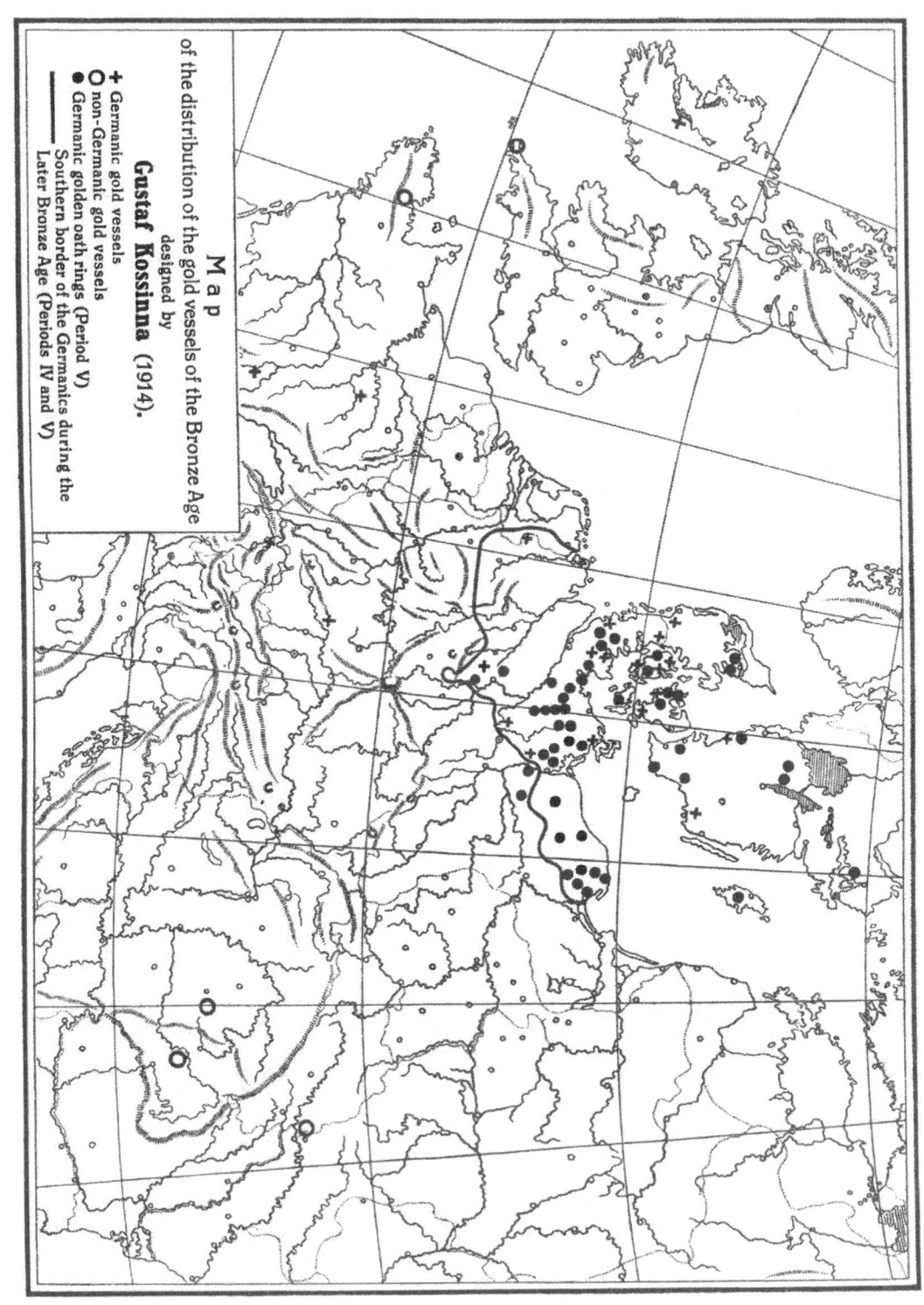

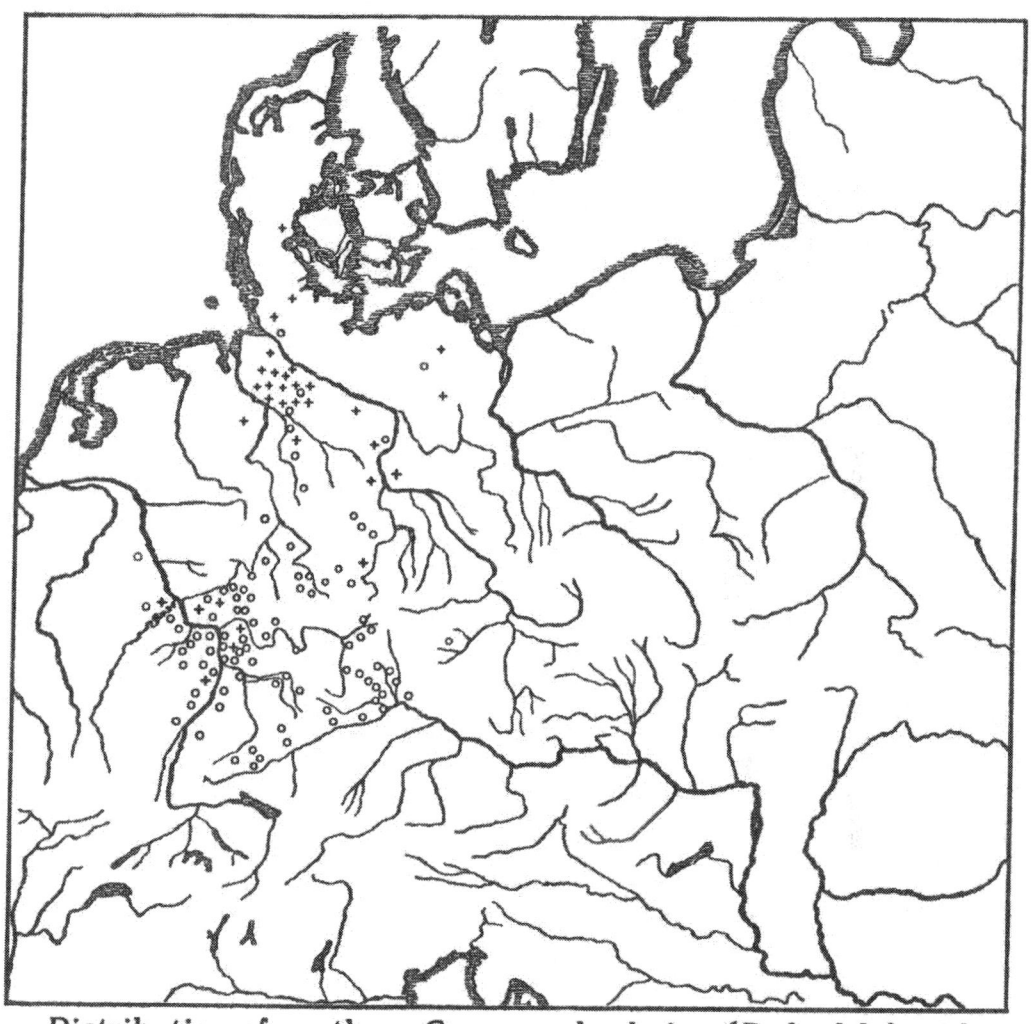

Distribution of southern German wheel pins (Radnadeln) with 1 eyelet (O) and of Hanoverian wheel pins with 3 eyelets (+). (Per Z. f. E. 1904, pp. 595 ff.)

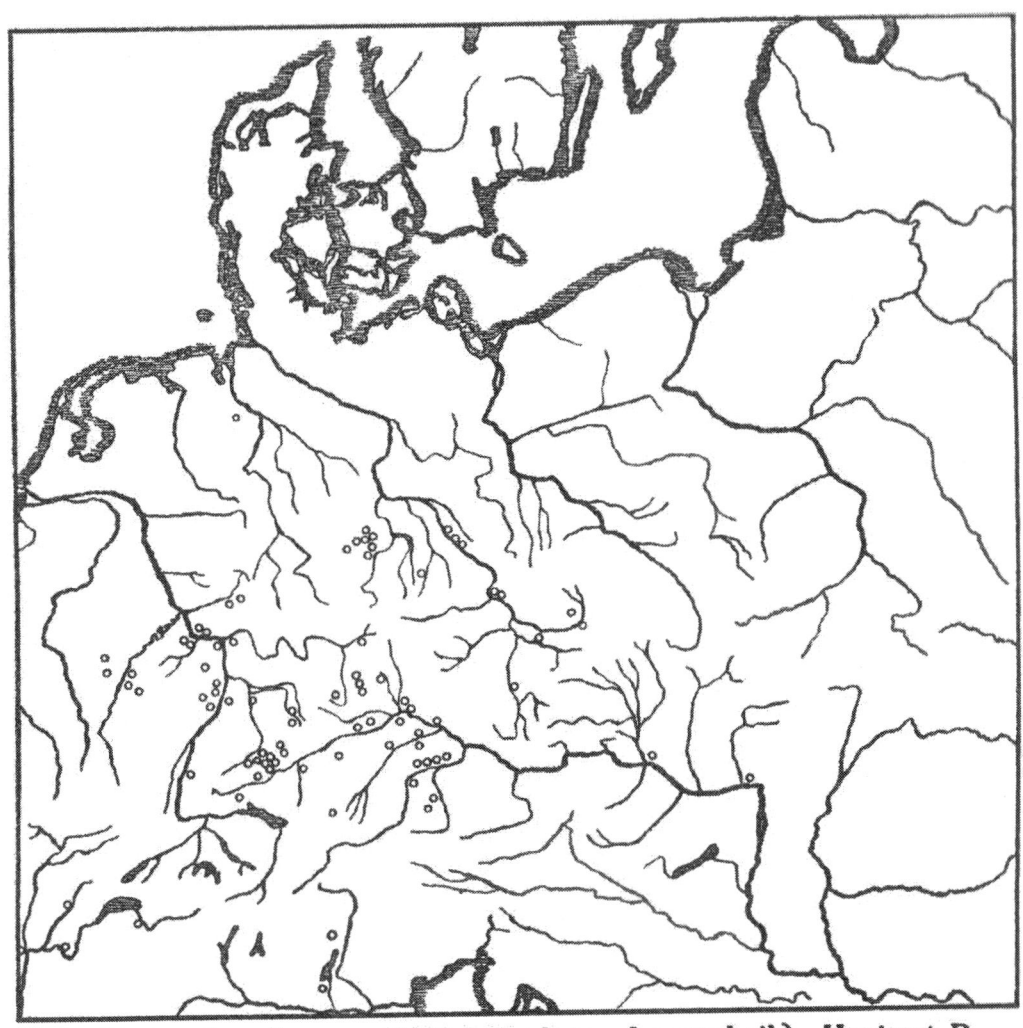

Median-winged axes (Mittelständiges Lappenbeil), Variant B;
Bronze Age Periods II c and III (1500—1200 BC)
(Per G. Wilke.)

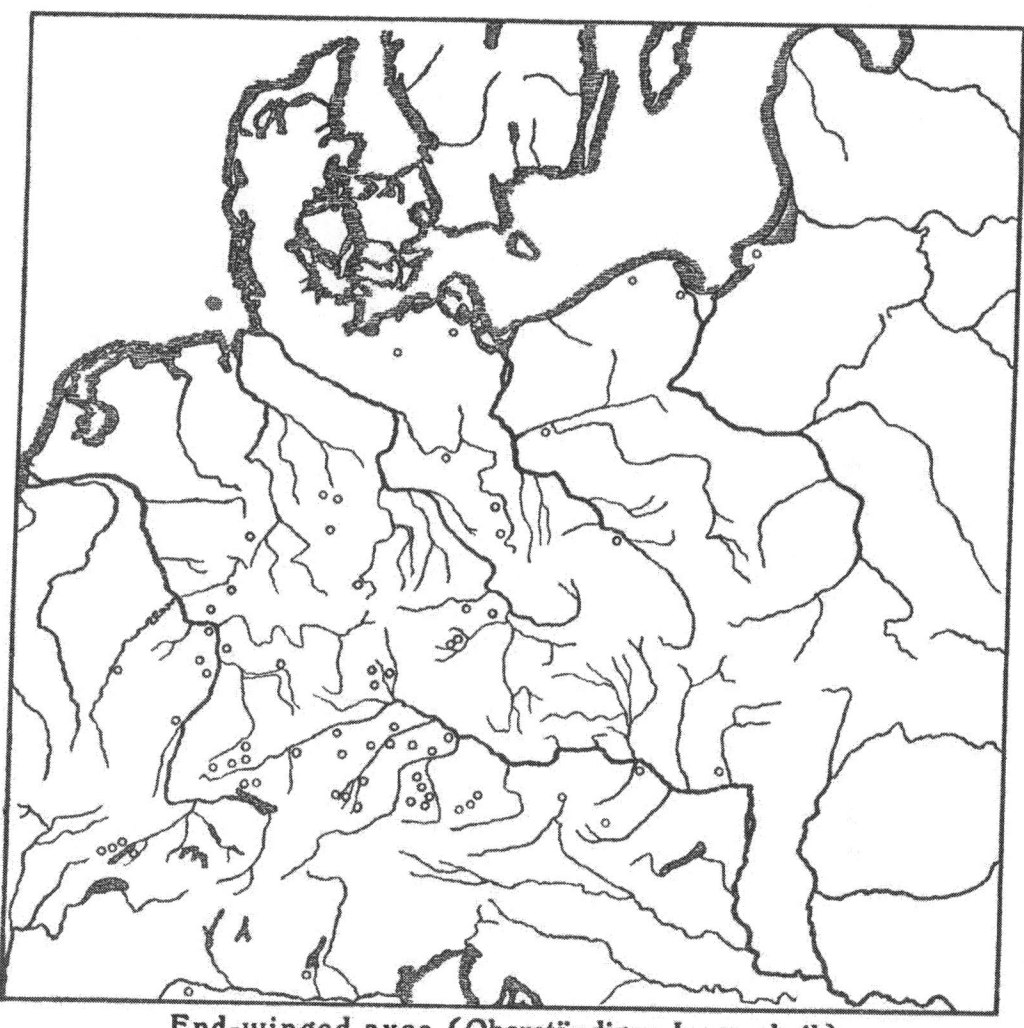

End-winged axes (Oberständiges Lappenbeil);
Bronze Age Periods IV—V (1150—750 BC)
(Per G. Wilke.)

Late La Tène fibulae, Variant K (120—1 BC)
(Per G. Wilke.)

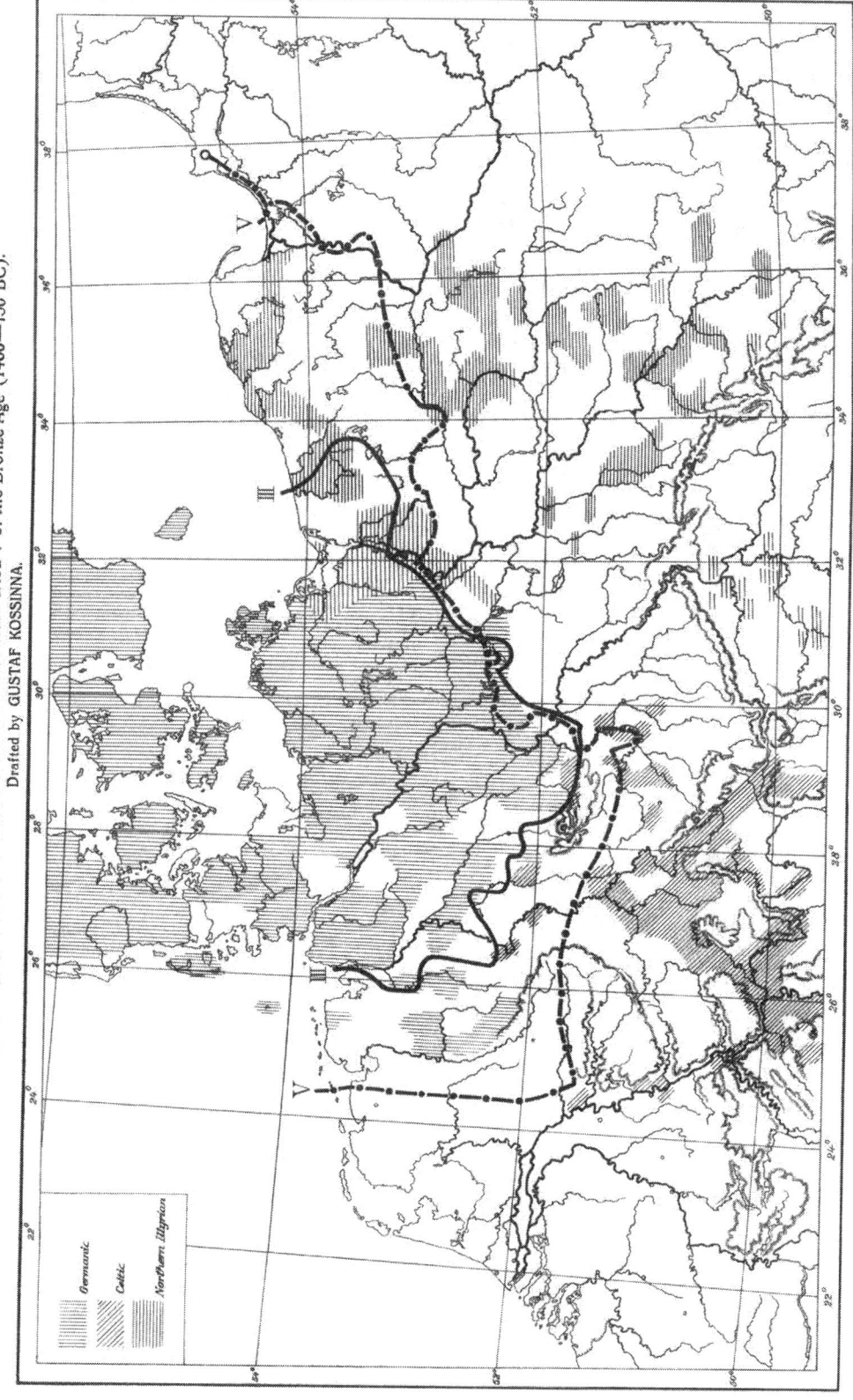

Settlement areas of the Germanics, Celts, and Northern Illyrians in Northern and Central Germany during Period II of the Bronze Age (1750—1400 BC) as well as the border of the Germanic area in Period III and Period V of the Bronze Age (1400—750 BC). Drafted by GUSTAF KOSSINNA.

ABOUT THE AUTHOR

Gustaf Kossinna was born in Tilsit, East Prussia on September 28, 1858, the son of a high school teacher. From 1876 to 1881 he studied at universities in Göttingen, Leipzig, Berlin, and Strasbourg, initially focusing on classical philology and then broadening his studies to include Germanic philology, art history, history, and archaeology. In 1881 he was awarded a doctorate by the Kaiser Wilhelm University of Strasbourg for his work on the oldest High Franconian language monuments in Strasbourg. It was his studies at the Friedrich Wilhelm University of Berlin under professor of Germanic philology Karl Müllenhoff that would inspire him to devote his career to prehistoric archaeology to pursue the origin of the Germanic people, and more broadly, the origin of the Indo-Europeans. After earning his doctorate, Kossinna spent several years as a librarian and then a curator at several libraries in Germany, and simultaneously began developing his archaeological method and publishing scientific papers. In May 1900 he was granted the title of professor by the same Berlin university where he had studied under Müllenhoff, but it was not until 1902 that he was appointed to an assistant professorship in German archaeology, a position created specifically for him.

After the death of German prehistorian Albert Voss in 1906, Kossinna had hoped to take his place as the director of the department of prehistory at the Royal Museums in Berlin, but in 1908 the position instead went to prehistorian Carl Schuchhardt, precipitating a rivalry between the two which would last for decades. When in 1909 Schuchhardt founded the journal *Prähistorische Zeitschrift* as an organ of the Berlin Society for Anthropology, Ethnology, and Prehistory, of which Kossinna was a member, Kossinna responded in the same year by founding the German Society for Prehistory (later renamed the Society for German Prehistory in 1913). The journal *Mannus* was then founded to serve as the organ of the new society, with Kossinna as editor. Kossinna would go on to write numerous publications on the prehistory of the Germanics and the Indo-Europeans before his death in Berlin on December 20, 1931. Through these publications and the development of his method of settlement archaeology, he played a seminal role in the emergence of prehistory as an academic discipline. His approach began to fall out of favor in the decades following World War II, but major advances in archaeogenetics have refocused scholarly discussion on prehistoric migrations, reviving interest in his legacy.

Made in the USA
Columbia, SC
27 September 2023